Routledge Revivals

English History in Forms of Essays

English History in Forms of Essays (1927) is an audacious and ambitious history of England in an abbreviated form of entries that both illuminate and provide openings for further research.

English History in Forms of Essays

Political and Constitutional 1066–1688

D.C. Cousins

First published in 1927
by George Allen & Unwin Ltd

This edition first published in 2025 by Routledge
4 Park Square, Milton Park, Abingdon, Oxon, OX14 4RN

and by Routledge
605 Third Avenue, New York, NY 10017

Routledge is an imprint of the Taylor & Francis Group, an informa business

© 1927 George Allen & Unwin Ltd

All rights reserved. No part of this book may be reprinted or reproduced or utilised in any form or by any electronic, mechanical, or other means, now known or hereafter invented, including photocopying and recording, or in any information storage or retrieval system, without permission in writing from the publishers.

Publisher's Note
The publisher has gone to great lengths to ensure the quality of this reprint but points out that some imperfections in the original copies may be apparent.

Disclaimer
The publisher has made every effort to trace copyright holders and welcomes correspondence from those they have been unable to contact.

A Library of Congress record exists under LCCN: 27023417

ISBN: 978-1-032-95571-1 (hbk)
ISBN: 978-1-003-58555-8 (ebk)
ISBN: 978-1-032-95573-5 (pbk)

Book DOI 10.4324/9781003585558

ENGLISH HISTORY IN FORMS OF ESSAYS

Political and Constitutional
1066–1688

For the Use of Students

By

D. C. COUSINS, M.A.
of New College, Oxford

LONDON
GEORGE ALLEN & UNWIN LTD
MUSEUM STREET

First published in 1927
(All rights reserved)

*Printed in Great Britain by
Unwin Brothers, Ltd., Woking*

FOREWORD

If the form of expression is, at least, as impressive as the matter handled, the reason for this method of presenting answers to conspicuous questions of English History will be obvious at a glance.

I can lay no claim to original research, and am therefore deeply indebted for information on the materials to a variety of authors read by me at different periods, and especially to the works of Alison, Buckle, Gardiner, Oman, Anson, Dicey, Maitland, May, Stubbs, and Taswell-Langmead.

It has often seemed to me to be rather doubtful whether the conventional style of book-writing—assuming the author's purpose to be educational—is the most perfect imaginable for effecting that purpose.

For students of exceptional ability, perhaps fifteen in a hundred, it has served well enough for centuries, for the reason that there is no abysmal difference between their intellectual fibre and that of the authors; but, to serve the student of average or modest intelligence as if he ranked with the exceptional, invites disappointment; and the delicacy of the compliment does not redeem the grossness of the fiction.

To a large proportion of students the unrelieved sameness of almost uniform type, in which causes, motives, purposes, results, great and trivial, are equally undistinguished to the eye, is apt to be fatiguing, and concentration flags; hence, the attraction, which works of profound merit have for the few, is non-existent for the many. One is reminded of the reflection of the Greek poet, that when the eye is unsupported all charm disappears: 'Ομμάτων δ'ἐν ἀχηνίαις ἔρρει πᾶσ' Ἀφροδίτα (Æschylus).

It must be within the experience of most teachers that there are numerous examinees, the motion of whose thoughts resembles, not the orderly well-spaced march of a regiment of Guards, but the misty meanderings of a huddled herd, quite ineffective for attack. Hence my adoption of a method in which, the fullest advantage being taken of the printer's art, an attempt is made to stimulate exercise in orderly thought, by exposure to the eye of distinctions, comparisons, and subordination of lesser to larger movements, motives, influences, and results.

But such a methodical survey should be only preparatory to a wider and deeper range of study, as a guide is used for ascent to high altitudes, or a chart by those who would explore the main It is therefore to be hoped that the student, who is moved by the new sensation of seeing his way in advance, will attack the more massive and masterly works with heightened anticipation, and amplify the outlines with detail, selecting such furnishings, curios, and refinements of historical learning as his, or her, own taste may fancy. The trite advice, that a student should "find out things for himself," is doubtless sound, if qualified with the proviso that he is first of all equipped with a method of search; else, the majority of those pitched

FOREWORD

into the "treasure-hunt" will draw blanks: only the few "born" researchers will be "winners."

In physical culture the enthusiast learns from some expert methods of muscular training, and practises them himself: the novice in art is led up to doing good work of his own by copying first from choice originals; so too, although no magic, no artistry of teaching, can save a student the trouble of taking exercise in reasoning, yet it is very possible, by exhibiting specimen forms of orderly thought, to attract him towards it, if his inclination is not spontaneous, or to intensify his zest, if it is.

My belief in the merits of such a method of study has been amply confirmed in recent years by assurances from former pupils, now very eminent in politics, law, and academic work, that the real aid they got from Oxford towards success in their life-work was not so much the matter learnt as the method by which they learnt it.

I understand there are those who may frown severely on the monstrous union of discordant species of type, to be noticed in this work; a well-observed tradition of the printer's art is violated.

I must confess that in this matter my resistance to the prayers and entreaties of my publishers has been adamantine; so the cumulative guilt, of insisting on another's sin, is entirely mine.

I can only plead, in mitigation, a passion for the extra-visible, and offer apologies to all who deprecate so profane a lapse of loyalty to the traditional.

D. C. COUSINS.

OXFORD, 1927.

MAGIS
VERITAS
OCULATA FIDE
QUAM PER AURES
ANIMIS HOMINUM
INFIGITUR.

(MODESTINUS)

An *asterisk* denotes that the topic is handled separately elsewhere in this work.

PERIOD I 1066–1272.

Normans and Angevins.

DESPOTISM—absolute and undisguised.

I. A **MONARCHY** of **vast power** is organised, against anarchy, by **William I, Henry I, Henry II**;

Administration is **CENTRALISED**
for *warfare, taxation, jurisdiction.*

Legislation on new *substantive* law is **rare**; but, on **procedure**, new rules are issued on the *initiative of the King*, or his judges.

But (a) The sceptre was too heavy for a *weak* king, too oppressive in the hands of a *tyrant.*

(b) The *hereditary* principle was *not* rooted, *as yet*, in our law; "**Election**" might oust it.

II. THAT MONARCHY was ∴ **THREATENED** with

A. **Extinction** or **Rivalry**—by the **BARONAGE**; i.e.,
  (i) Revolts *anarchical* by the *old* feudatories.
  (ii) Movements *constitutional* by the *new* barons.

B. **Division** of its supremacy—by the **CHURCH**; was Church to be *co-ordinate* with State?

C. **Limits** on absolutism—by **VOX POPULI.**

"**Magna Carta**" was won by these 3 co-operating;

"**Provisions of Oxford**" 1258 embodied on paper a *Baronial oligarchy*; but the Monarchy, which overcame A and B, **yielded,** without great pressure, **to C.**

III. A NATIONAL PARLIAMENT

∴ takes shape in the 13th century; for

The Conditions were favourable to a precocious growth of English "**NATIONALITY**," i.e., a sense
  of the organic unity of our State:
  of our common ideals, traditions, and interests:
  of our detachment from foreign Powers:—

viz. (1) **English Feudalism**—a *consolidating* force;
  (2) **Fusion** *rapid* of Normans and English;
  (3) **Homogeneity** of our *Counties* and *Towns*;
  (4) **A Common Law,** fostered by itinerant Judges;
  (5) Our **Insular position**; and the loss of the French duchies, making our *Barons* more exclusively *English.*
  (6) Our **Antipathy** to **aliens,** so aggravated under Henry III.

WILLIAM I 1066—1087.

His claim :—In fact rested on **Conquest,** and **Witan's** election; but he professed to be *Heir* by the Confessor's *nomination,* though

(i) the nearest "*Heir*" was Edgar Atheling;

and (ii) "*nomination*" by a late King was no title.

His aim :—To weld Normans and English into

One CENTRALISED State ;

Himself to be its active, irresponsible, **Head**— a **Rightful King** of even the humblest of the Conquered, not merely Captain of the invaders.

HIS POLICY ?

I. As CONQUEROR, and KING of the ENGLISH :—

(a) **against the REBELS**—he played the **Conqueror,** reducing each in turn, e.g. *Edwin, Morcar, Hereward*;

(i) **Lands confiscated** were in some cases **re-granted** to old owners, who ∴ *admitted his Lordship.*

(ii) **Norman Castles** were built to overawe them.

(iii) **Palatine Earldoms** secured the **borders,** i.e. of *Durham, Chester, Kent,* to which he delegated vice-regal powers over a County.

(b) **towards PEACEFUL SUBJECTS**—he posed as carrying on a **legitimate Kingship ;**

∴ (i) "**Laws of Edward**" he expressly confirmed; *but* some Norman practices he imported for Norman use, e.g. "*Wager of Battle.*"

(ii) **Local** English **institutions** he retained, *e.g.* the *Fyrd,* and *Courts* of Sheriff and Hundred; *but* these were to be in touch with his Central authority.

(iii) **The Witan** survived; *but* he feudalised it into a Court of *tenants-in-chief.*

II. As **DUKE** of the **NORMANS :**—he imported a **FEUDALISM qualified ;** for whereas

in *France*—**Feudalism** was a system both

A. **of TENURE**—with exceptions ("*allodial*" titles); for services hardly so oppressive as here; tenants owing fealty to *immediate lords*; and

B. of GOVERNMENT—by provincial Dukes or Counts, whose **Domains** were **compact,** undispersed; held by *Prescription*, not by royal Grant;

and whose **Independence** was shown in their control of *military forces, jurisdiction, taxation,* and *coinage*;

∴ the *French* King had only a *vague suzerainty*, such feudalism being a "*centrifugal*" force, making for *provincialism*, not State solidarity ;—

into *England*—**William imported A,** *excluding B*;

∴ **A. By the AGENCY of SUBSERVIENT NORMANS,** the principle of **TENURE** was applied without exceptions, **THE LAND** being a foundation on which to elaborate not a "patchwork" but **Manors** and sub-tenancies multiplied on the *same pattern*, with some fancy **vice-royalties** for the borders. Thus

I. FEUDALISM was EXTENDED ∴

to the **Personal** tie created by "*Commendation*," by which a Saxon *allodial* owner swore fidelity to, expecting protection from, the local chief, he added a **Territorial** bond, i.e.,

(a) **Tenancy** was made universal: "*allodium*" ceased:

(b) **Manors** replaced Saxon free villages:

(c) **Services,** especially *military*, were made the condition of all landholding:

(d) **Jurisdiction** *territorial* became incident to lordship, overlordship, to Kingship above all.

II. CONSTITUTIONAL RESULTS were:—a **new type** of **Sovereignty**—∴ *Centralised*; and *Territorial*, i.e. embracing all the land, ∴ *all within it*, irrespective of their personality; hence a new basis for

    (1) **Allegiance,**   (2) **Jurisdiction,**

of **Common Council**—∴ the *Witan* was changed into a court of *Tenants-in-chief*.

of **Aristocracy,** ∴ of Landlords.

of **Military force,** ∴ Feudal Array.

of **Revenue system,** ∴ Feudal Dues. But

B. Against any REFRACTORY BARONS—who might sigh for the *governing* powers of Dukes of France—he **FORTIFIED THE CROWN,** *preventing French feudalism taking root here*, by

I. Express grants to Barons, as *servants* to be *rewarded*, not of compact domains, but of **Manors Dispersed,**

∴ (a) *attackable* by the King at many points; and a baron could *not readily concentrate* his forces;

∴ (b) Barons were the readier to *combine inter se.*

II. Abolition of the old earldoms, which had divided England, and might become *imperia in imperio*.

III. **Oath of Salisbury 1086**—exacted even from sub-vassals, *direct to the King*; ∴ it would be *Treason*, if they fought, for their mesne lords, against King.

IV. **English local** authorities being **confirmed,** e.g. Sheriffs ∴ Barons could not monopolise local power.

V. **Church** being **strengthened,** as the Crown's ally.*

VI. **Pre-eminence** being **assured to the CROWN,** as to

(a) *Landed wealth* :—

∴ folcland he appropriated as " Terra Regis ";
1,400 Manors he reserved for his own;
chief Towns also he held " *in demesne.*"

(b) *Sporting rights* :—in the royal **Forests,** which he extended and rigidly preserved.

(c) *Taxation* :—∴ he had " **Doomsday** " **survey** made, as a basis for assessment.

(d) *Jurisdiction* :—∴ all local courts were subordinated to his *Curia Regis.*

Thus **KINGSHIP** in England was secured as a **REAL, effective, SOVEREIGNTY.** Feudalism here was a **Centralising, Consolidating** force, tending to *Organic Unity* of the State.

WILLIAM'S POLICY TOWARDS THE CHURCH?

I. **He strengthened it for alliance** with Crown;

(a) Church **Courts** to be **Separate,** and apply Canon law; previously Bishop sat with Sheriff.

(b) **Norman clerics,** e.g. *Lanfranc,* held the sees, though minor clergy were English;
so Church came into contact with learning and spirit of Christendom, and became the " nursery of statesmen."

(c) **Monastic system** was encouraged, e.g. celibacy.

but II. **King's** authority to be **supreme**

∴ (1) *Homage to Pope* he refused.

(2) Its *lands* he *taxed* for military service.

(3) Not without King's sanction was

a *Baron* to be *excommunicated*
a *Canon* to be *enacted*
a *Papal* legate or letter *recognised.*

HOW FAR DID WILLIAM'S POLICY EMBARRASS his SUCCESSORS?

(1) **Sheriff's Office** became hereditary, usurped by Barons, oppressive; ∴ Hen: I, Hen: II had to put in *new men.*

(2) **Church separation** led to a dream of Church *supremacy*; n.b. Becket and Henry II.

(3) **Forests** were a sharp reminder of tyranny; made Crown odious under Hen: I, Hen: II.

(4) **Palatine Earldoms**—too great a devolution of royal powers; became centres of revolt by
> e.g. in 1074 Earls of Hereford and Norfolk;
> in 1173 Hugh de Puiset of Durham, etc.,

but indirectly drove Crown to *court* the support of *the People*.

GENERAL RESULTS of NORMAN CONQUEST?

I. Political Power was redistributed
(though the *form of Constitution* was *unchanged*).
- (a) Central executive far stronger.
- (b) New Aristocracy developed.
- (c) Feudalism was developed, yet qualified.*

II. Church was brought into touch with Europe and Papacy;
∴ *disputes* of later Kings with Church and Pope: our Knights were drawn to *Crusades*.

III. Fusion of Two Races;
Norman laws, manners, language were imported: to solid virtues of Saxons were added Norman ideals of chivalry and adaptability.

IV. England lost her isolation;
Our Kings became claimants to half France.
∴ long *wars* v. France: ∴ foreign *alliances* were sought.

HENRY II 1154—1189.

The first of the "**Angevins**" (*Henry II, Richard I, John, Henry III*).

POLITICAL INFLUENCES during his reign?

A. **Precedents** set by Henry I.
   How far did Henry II carry on his grandfather's policy?
   1. Charter reissued.
   2. Foreign alliances.
   3. Administrative system recast.
   4. Resistance to the Church and Pope.
   5. Middle class men raised to office.
   but more of a *Legislator*, and he had *Imperial ambitions*.

B. **Church**—too predominant under Stephen—now had **to be curbed**.

C. **Barons' final effort** for feudal independence.

D. **Queen Eleanor's** bad influence.
   ∴ Rebellions of his sons, backed by France.

E. **3rd Crusade 1188**.
   ∴ 1. More contact with *foreigners*.
   2. *Turbulent spirits* were drawn off.
   3. *Need of money* ∴ new sort of tax, i.e. "*Saladin tithe*"; and a bargain with Scotland.
   4. Field for *chivalry*: so national character was elevated by Knightly ideals.

HENRY II's POLICY?

A. His **IMPERIAL AMBITIONS** extended to
   I. **British Isles** ∴ he attacked *Wales*; half subdued *Ireland*; made William of *Scotland* do homage.
   II. **French possessions**:—he had Normandy: Anjou, Maine, Touraine: Aquitaine;
   and designs on Toulouse and Brittany.
   ∴ (a) *Diplomatic Marriages* of
   himself with Eleanor of Aquitaine.
   his son Geoffrey—Constance of Brittany.
   his son Henry—Margaret of France.
   (b) *Alliances* with Spain, Sicily, Saxony.
   (c) His *long absences* ∴ despotism less felt at home; Justiciars (De Lucy; and Glanvil) governed.
   (d) "*Scutage*" first in Toulouse war ∴ mercenaries could be bought.
   (e) *Patronage* of literary men, to win prestige abroad.
   But his continental schemes were **thwarted** by
   (1) Hereditary rivalries of French provinces.
   (2) Want of a national bond.
   (3) Enmity of King Philip.
   (4) Rebellions of his sons.

B. HIS CONSTITUTIONAL REFORMS :—

General aims ?

To **correct** the **anarchy** of Stephen's reign ;

∴ The **King's Law** must be **supreme** over *Church* ;

The **King's Law** must be **supreme** in the *State* ;

∴ **Baronial power** must be **reduced :**

∴ (a) Crown's *Military* resources must be independent of the Barons ;
 (b) Crown's *Revenue* must be enriched ;
 (c) *Justice* to be administered on new lines, with the King for its fountain-head, and Justices in eyre as distributors of an
 (d) *Uniform Common Law*, superseding locally variable customs.

The FORMS of his LEGISLATION ?

I. By **Charter**, declaratory, he ratified that of Henry I, e.g. as to Church's liberties.

II. By **Constitutions of Clarendon** 1164 :—

After his quarrel with Becket over (1) Trial of Criminal Clerics, (2) Church lands' liability to Danegeld ;

(a) The *King's Court* to have primary jurisdiction as to Cleric's crimes, Advowsons, Land disputes between clergy and laymen. Bishops' Courts were not to screen a criminal cleric.
(b) *Appeals ecclesiastical* to lie not to Rome, but to Bishop, then to Archbishop, then to King.
(c) *Vacant Sees* to be in King's custody ; and Church lands held in capite are liable as baronies.
(d) *Not* without the *King's assent* may
   (i) a *new* Bishop be *elected* ; and such election must be in the King's Chapel.
   (ii) a Tenant-in-chief be *excommunicated*.
   (iii) a Cleric *leave England*.

These provisos were revoked after Becket's murder ; but they anticipated the 1534 " Reformation " ; and the predominance of the King's Court in fact persisted.

III. By various **Assizes** :—esp. :

The " *Grand* " *Assize*—introduced a civil Jury ; v.i.

Assize of Clarendon 1166

   (i) Circuits of Judges to be more regular :
   (ii) Jury of " Presentment," i.e. 12 from each hundred, to accuse reputed criminals ;
      ∴ trial by " Ordeal " to follow.
   (iii) Sheriffs' duties particularised : e.g. to review " Frankpledge " : hunt down criminals, etc.

Assize of Northampton 1176

   (a) Duties of Judges on circuit further defined—to exact King's dues, and oath of fealty, etc.
   (b) Possessory Assizes to be held by royal Commissioners ; v.i.
   (c) Accused, if " Ordeal " went against him, to be mutilated ; if in his favour, may be required to abjure the realm.

Assize of Arms 1181 ; v.i.

THE **REFORMS** COMPASSED by Henry II?

A. ROYAL JURISDICTION, as to cases of first instance, was **ENLARGED,**

   for **King's Bench,** which he specialised as 5 Judges 1178, for jurisdiction criminal and (until 1215) civil;

   for **Justices in eyre,** whose circuits, started by Henry I, but lapsing under Stephen, were now revived with wider powers.

To such jurisdiction he **SUBORDINATED**

  I. **Church Courts**—see *Constitutions of Clarendon.*

  II. *Barons'* **Manorial Courts**—

    ∴ (a) "*Writ of Right*" from the King to the lord (that he do justice to A) must issue *before* a Court Baron could try A's claim v. B to freehold ownership.

    (b) "*Writ of Præcipe*" from King to Sheriff—that he order X, e.g. to pay his debt to Y, else to summon X before the King's Justice—might divert the case from the Lord's Court.

    (c) Assizes of *Novel Disseisin*, and *Mort d'ancestor*, (as to land possession) and of *Darrien Presentment*, (as to advowsons)—to be tried only by the King's Commissioners, *no longer* by *Lord's* Court.

  III. *Sheriff's* **County Courts**—

   these being made more servient to the Justices in eyre, whom the Sheriffs were to meet "with their counties."

B. JUDICIAL PROCEDURE was improved by JURIES,
    a "*regale beneficium*," according to Glanvil;

  I. for **Trial** of **Civil** suits as to **Land :**—

   (a) If *Writ of Right* by A v. B,
   B was to have, instead of *Wager of Battle*, option of a "**Grand Assize**," i.e. A and B chose 4 knights, who chose 12 others, who decided even the question of *right*.

   (b) If Assize of *Novel Disseisin*, *etc.*—the Writ told Sheriff to summon 12, who, as a "*Petty Assize*," found on the question of *fact*, e.g. was there a wrongful disseisin, or not?

  II. for **Initiating** process v. a reputed **Criminal B :**—

   i.e. to supersede "*Compurgation*"

    (by which B, the accused, had got e.g. 12 others to swear to the value of B's oath of innocence),

   and to supplement, now that Crime was becoming a matter of *social* import, the "*Appeal of Felony*"

    (by which A, for e.g. murder of A's sister, sought *private* vengeance v. B, who could demand "*Battle*," until 1819),

   a **Jury of Presentment** (12) was to be summoned by Sheriff for each county and hundred; this **Grand Jury** shall accuse B before a Justice in eyre; then B must go for *trial* by "*Ordeal*" of water.

- **C. MILITARY FORCES?** The King was made more *independent* of the Baronage;
  - ∴ **I. Feudal Array** was degraded by *Scutage*, which enabled him to buy Mercenaries for foreign wars;
    - **II. Fyrd**, i.e. County Militia, was revived 1181 by *Assize of Arms* :—every man to provide arms according to his income as *assessed by local juries*; such arms to descend to heirs, ∴ inalienable. Hence a force which King could rely upon in riot, rebellion, or invasion.

- **D. REVENUE and TAXATION?**
  - Crown was enriched by enlargement of the royal **Jurisdiction**; and by **Scutage**.
  - The "**Saladin Tithe**" 1188, on personal wealth, to be assessed by juries, introduced a new species of Direct Tax.

- **Henry's ANTI-BARONIAL measures** summarised :—
  - (1) Royal **encroachment** on Manorial **jurisdiction**: v.s.
  - (2) Resumption of **royal demesnes** conferred by Stephen on his barons; and razing the adulterine castles.
  - (3) "**Inquest of Sheriffs**" 1170;—to stop abuses of Shrievalties, esp. by barons who had annexed the office for the chances it offered of extortion; all were ejected, some restored, many new men put in as servants of Crown.
  - (4) "**Scutage**": and "**Assize of Arms**"; v.s.

- **N.B. Two famous works** throw light on this reign :—
  - "**Dialogus de Scaccario**" 1177, by Fitzneal, Bishop and Treasurer, as to Exchequer business, sources of Revenue, how it was collected, and accounts checked.
  - "**Glanvil's**" **Tractatus** on "*laws and customs*" of England :—describes the work of the Royal Courts: declines to tell the vast variety of local customs, which uniform Common Law was beginning to supersede. Possibly written by the Justiciar Glanvil 1187.

CONSTITUTIONAL MOVEMENTS
of the 13th Century?

I. **MAGNA CARTA 1215.**

II. **Barons' plans** for *limiting the Monarchy* :—
   Some would do so by **OLIGARCHY**:
   See "*Provisions of Oxford*" 1258;
   Montfort preferred **POPULAR REPRESENTATION.**

III. **Edward I's policy**
   RE-FOUNDING the **MONARCHY**:
   forming a **NATIONAL PARLIAMENT**, with an eye to more productive *Taxation*.

MAGNA CARTA 1215.

EVENTS LEADING UP to it?

King John had a weak position after his quarrel with *Church*, and with *Barons*: his tyranny over all: his submission to the Pope: his reverses in France;

Prelates, and **Barons,** in contrast with earlier baronage, *more English,* in sympathy, after loss of French duchies; *more imbued,* by official status, with a spirit of *Law* and *Order,* rejected John's offer of preferential concessions to them, and, by voicing the grievances of *all,* secured liberties for *all.*

ITS HISTORICAL INTEREST?

I. Some **national solidarity** is proved by its achievement.

II. A **standard of legalism** was erected to which future **Reformers** could appeal; and by which future **Kings** were reminded that *royal power* here was *fettered*;
so the *fact* of its erection was even more vital than the substance of most of its provisions.

III. Our **national Parliament** was formed by the struggle for its maintenance; there were 4 editions, 1215, 1216, 1217, 1225; and the nation paid future Kings to **Re-affirm** it at numerous dates, ending 1424.

MAIN PROVISIONS
of Magna Carta 1215.

Drawn from Edward the Confessor's Laws: Henry I's Charter: Henry II's reforms; ∴ mostly traditional, but *some new.**

A. For the **CHURCH**—" Anglicana Ecclesia libera sit ";
e.g. as to Election of bishops, and Self-taxation.

B. For the **BARONS** and their **TENANTS**—

*(1) **No Scutage,** or extraordinary **Aid,** to be levied without the consent of the *Common Council*; to form which,

(2) **Greater barons** shall be summoned by *individual writ* to each; **Lesser barons,** by *writ to Sheriff.*
The vote of those attending shall bind absentees.
(1) (2) are omitted in later editions.

*(3) **Writ Præcipe** shall no longer issue so as to withdraw a land suit from the lord's court.

(4) **Reliefs,** i.e. duties paid by adult heirs, shall be *fixed.*

(5) **Widows** of tenants to have their *Dower,* and are *not* to be *forced* to re-marry.

C. For **TRADERS**—

(a) **Alien merchants** in *peace* are to travel free from maletotes; but in *war* may be detained as hostages.

(b) **London,** and other **Towns,** to retain their ancient privileges.

(c) **Weights and Measures** shall be *uniform.*

(d) **Purveyance** shall be conditional on payment for the goods commandeered.

D. For ALL SUBJECTS—JUSTICE : ∴

(i) **No freeman** shall be imprisoned, disseised, or in any way destroyed . . . **unless**

    (a) "*per judicium parium*"— ∴ e.g. a baron by barons', a freeholder by freeholders', judgment ;

or (b) "*by law of the land*"—e.g. if Wager of Battle.

(ii) **To no man** will we **sell, delay,** or **deny,** Justice.

(iii) **Fines** to be measured by the offence, not by the offender's means ; and *not* to be levied on his *means of livelihood*, not e.g. on a Villein's implements.

(iv) **Assizes** of **Novel Disseisin, etc.**—to be heard 4 times a year, by 2 Justices and 4 Knights, in each county.

*(v) **No Sheriff**, or castle-Constable, to hear "**Placita Corone.**"

*(vi) "**Communia Placita,**" i.e. *civil* cases, shall *no longer* "*follow*" the King's Court, but be heard in "*some fixed place.*"

*(vii) **Writ** "**de odio et atiâ**" shall issue *gratis*, as of *right* ;

∴ X could be released by Sheriff on bail, if detained maliciously on charge of homicide.

SECURITY PROVIDED for **observance** of the Charter ?

By § 61 **legalised rebellion :**—25 *elected Barons*, after notice of breach to the King, and 40 days default of redress, shall, *with the Commonalty* (they being *liable to swear obedience to the* 25) *distrain* on the King's possessions, and *distress* him in any way, short of personal harm to the Royal family.

29

HENRY III 1216—1272.

A. **His Minority** (∵ aged 9) ∴ **MINISTERS** ruled :—

   William the Marshal :—
   drove out Louis after "*Lincoln Fair*" and "*Treaty Lambeth*"; re-issued Magna Carta; issued also "Charter of the Forest" 1217, relaxing the law.

   Peter des Roches :—
   King's tutor, and leader of the *foreign* clique.

   Hubert de Burgh :—a commoner: Justiciar till 1232.
   (1) *Advocate of Henry II's system*
       ∴ he attacked some turbulent Barons, took Bedford castle, hanged the garrison.
   (2) *Ardent Patriot* — "he restored England to England" :—
       he ousted the foreigners, des Roches, de Bréauté.
       beat French fleet in the Channel.
       deprecated Henry's designs on France.
       resisted Papal tyranny and exactions.
       but 1232 was upset by des Roches, and persecuted.

B. **EVILS of the ADMINISTRATION? Need of Reforms?**
   I. **Foreigners** swarmed, even in State offices.
   ∴ II. **Extortions** esp. by **Talliages** (on towns on demesnes of King) for Court luxury, favourites, and foreign designs.
   III. **Ministers irresponsible ;**
        no popular Assembly to criticise them or voice grievances.
   IV. **Pope's** domination * demoralised the Church, split it from the laity, and drained away money.
   V. **Justice difficult** ∵ Bench servile to Crown: Sheriffs abused their offices: Local Courts feared strong offenders.

C. **SIMON DE MONTFORT and the movement for REFORM :**
   Of French origin, but Earl of Leicester on his mother's side; here 1230, a Court favourite, married King's sister; but offended King by antipathy to Pope; went on Crusade: later ruled Gascony, and on return led the

   BARONS' opposition to HENRY :—

   Two conflicting aims in this, though *both* meant *limits on Monarchy*).
   I. **Feudal**—i.e. of Richard of Gloucester's party, in favour of an *Oligarchy* of Barons, a fettered King, a nation of serfs.
   II. **Popular**—preferred by Montfort (backed by the Towns, inspired by teaching of Friars, e.g. Grosseteste and Adam Marisco), who wished *all the Nation* to be consulted by the King.

   1254 **2 Knights** from each *shire* were summoned, in Henry's absence, to discuss an "aid."

1258 "**Mad Parliament**" of **Barons,** at which a **Council of 24** was named (12 by *King*, 12 by *Barons*).

"**PROVISIONS OF OXFORD**" issued by this, created a permanent **Council of 15,** chosen by 2 of the King's 12, and 2 of the Barons' 12.

(i) To control King and appoint ministers.
(ii) To invent remedies for special abuses.
(iii) To consult thrice a year with *12 elected Barons.*

Sworn to by King and prince Edward.

But too **elaborate,** and **oligarchic ;** and, though Alien wardens of royal castles were driven out, the Council of 15 was slow to invent other remedies.

∴ on pressure from **Knights,** appealing to **Edward,**

1259 "**Provisions of Westminster**"
specified remedies in regard to e.g. Forests : Sheriff to be checked by 4 knights : of 4, elected in shire court, Barons of Exchequer to nominate one as Sheriff.

But Henry chafed at the **1258** "**Provisions,**" and hoped for a split in the Baronial party; Montfort did break with Gloucester in 1259 ; and in

1261 **3 Knights** from each *shire* were summoned by Montfort to St. Albans, by Henry to Windsor. 1262 Gloucester died ; and in 1263, on Montfort asking King to *confirm the Provisions,* his refusal led to

THE BARONS' WAR :—

(1) By "**Mise of Amiens**" 1264, *Louis IX* arbitrated in Henry's favour, against the Provisions.
But Montfort, after all, rejected the award.

∴ (2) **Battle of Lewes** 1264, won by Montfort and Londoners ; Then by "**Mise of Lewes**" Henry was required
to observe the *Charters.*
to dismiss all *foreign officials.*
to govern by a *Council of 9,* chosen by 3 barons.
Montfort kept Henry captive, and seized all revenues.

(3) **MONTFORT'S PARLIAMENT 1265**—to this he summoned some *Barons*—but only of his own party : 2 *Knights* from each *shire* (by writ to Sheriff)
and—by writs to *Cities* and *Boroughs*—2 *representatives* each ; ∴ *trade* was represented.

but (4) 1265 at Evesham—won by prince Edward—Montfort was killed. He had lost credit by his cruelty and arrogance : and his greed made Gilbert of Gloucester his foe. Yet, after death, he was by many deemed a saint.

(5) 1266 by "**Dictum de Kenilworth**"
Henry annulled the Provisions, and all Montfort's acts ; Crown was declared all powerful.

ADMINISTRATIVE SYSTEM.

NORMAN and ANGEVIN.

The King was absolutely and actively supreme; the **ORGANS** of his will being

A. **MINISTERS** of State—his nominees:—

- I. **Justiciar** (until Edw: I)—prime minister, viceroy, president of Justice, usually a cleric.
- II. **Chancellor**—King's secretary and chief chaplain; kept the great seal, issued writs and royal grants; superseded Justiciar under Edw: I.
- III. **Treasurer**—kept the treasure at Winchester: sat in the Exchequer: and had some jurisdiction from 1240 c. A few minor offices were *hereditary* esp. those of the **Marshal** and **High Constable**. **Sheriffs** were the *local* officials of most importance.

B. **COMMITTEES** of the **Great Council** *

- (1) *Concilium Ordinarium*, a consultative body.*
- (2) *Curia regis*—which specialised Jurisdiction, and followed the King.
- (3) *Exchequer*—for Finance, under special "*Barons*," and from 1230 c. a "*Chancellor*."

The **FUNCTIONS** were

- I. **Military,** i.e. the levy and control of Fyrd, Feudal array, Mercenaries, by the Marshal, the Constable, the Sheriffs.
- II. **Financial,** i.e. twice a year Exchequer sat to receive monies from Sheriffs, check accounts, and enter records on "*Pipe-Rolls.*"
- III. **Judicial**
   - (a) By *Local* Courts of Shire, Manor, Hundred, Township; but, as jurisdiction was lucrative, and Barons had to be curbed, these were linked with and limited
   - (b) By the *King's own* organs of Justice, i.e.
      - (i) *Standing* Courts, branching from the Council;
         - "**King's Bench**"—followed the King: heard appeals, cases of tenants-in-chief, and, by Henry II's reform, many others:
         - "**Common Pleas**" **Court**—fixed at Westminster after 1215, for *civil* suits.
         - "**Exchequer**"—which developed a jurisdiction as to *taxes* under Henry III.
      - (ii) *Justices* periodically commissioned for an "*Iter*," for fiscal work, trial of crime, or, by Henry II's plan, for possessory Assizes.

CHURCH and STATE

in 11th, 12th, 13th centuries;

Our relations with the Papacy?

Before the Conquest—**Harmonious** intercourse;
so King and Earls sat in Church Councils,
Bishops sat in County Courts, and in Witan;
No Papal aggression.

After the Conquest :—

A. UNION was WEAKENED because—

Though high ecclesiastics were ministers of State: and William I * aimed at binding Church to Crown: and Kings asked Popes to sanction enterprises, and owed, *some* their election, *all* their coronation, to the Church—

Yet I. Its closer touch with **Rome,** separate **Courts,** and **Convocation's** ancient privileges, tended to disunion; ∴ Henry I had to challenge Pope on *Investiture* of bishops, whose *military following* made their fealty to Crown a vital matter.

II. **In Stephen's anarchy** Church assumed a paramount power; ∴ a theory of *Church supremacy* was entertained ∴

B. QUARRELS of Church with State under

(a) **Henry II *** —with Becket; but King revoked the "Constitutions"; ∴ relations to Pope were left undefined.

(b) **John *** —who, after a long defiance of Pope and Bishops, made a degrading submission;

∴ "*Freedom*" of the Church heads Magna Carta, and

C. POPE was AGGRESSIVELY PREDOMINANT under **Henry III,** demanding *tribute*, "providing" *livings*, hearing *appeals*; this tended to divorce clerics from the King and laity: so the Church became

(i) *Detached—un-English*—worked by foreigners: which provoked **de Burgh's *** resistance to Pope.

(ii) *Lethargic*, and prelates too political: this stirred the **Friars' movement ***

∴ many clergy supported Montfort.

D. To bring ALL THE CHURCH within his **Political Scheme**—was Edward I's purpose;

∴ (1) He limited its abnormal wealth by Mortmain law.

(2) He called to his Model Parliament representatives even of the *lower* clergy.

(3) He taxed it; and 1296 *outlawed* clerics who stood by Pope Boniface's Bull "**Clericis laicos**" (Church revenues not to be taxed for Temporal Power).

POLITICAL INFLUENCES
of 13th CENTURY.

I. **Papal interference,** *
Splitting Clerics from Laity, Church from State.

II. **Loss of the French duchies :—**
1. *Forfeited*, said Philip, when John would not answer to him for murder of Arthur, and seizure of Isabel, the betrothed of Count de la Marche.

∴ 2. Norman *Barons sided with Philip*; John's resistance was feeble : Chateau Gaillard fell : we lost all *except Channel Isles and Lower Aquitaine* **1204.**

POLITICAL RESULTS of the loss ?
  (a) Growth of English **Unity :** antipathy to foreigners : fusion of Normans and English more rapid.
  (b) Our **Kings** more **resident** here—had to face their subjects, ∴ more criticism, *or* loyalty.
  (c) Our **Barons** more purely **English ;** the feudal obligation of service was weakened ; they demand, after Bouvines, Magna Carta (old *English* rules chiefly).
  (d) **Henry III** aspired to regain the duchies ; ∴ *courted foreigners* ; hence, by reaction,
    (i) Hubert de Burgh's patriotic movement : *
    (ii) Edward I's purely English monarchy.*

III. **Foreign** leanings of Henry III ;
∴ Aliens here in high places ;
Costly ambitions abroad, e.g. his designs on Sicily.
So a spirit of *Patriotism* was roused,
  a cry of " *England for the English.*"

IV. **Friars'** political teaching * : v.i.
i.e. *Vox populi* should be heard in government.

V. **Towns'** advance
  (a) in *Wealth* ∴ home trade prospered, esp. in wool, leather, cloth ; foreign trade was expanding, e.g. with Flanders and Bordeaux.
  Edward I was very sensible of the importance of Merchants, as a source of revenue, and a factor in politics.
  (b) in *Intelligence* : the Friars stirred political criticism ;
∴ (c) in *the spirit of Freedom*—helped by charters of incorporation, giving communal rights.
  So the Towns supported Montfort, and obtained *representation in Parliament.*

VI. Feudalism waning ;
> **Barons** of the old **feudal** type, hopeless now of *Local* independence, tried to absorb the *Central* power;
> while the Official Nobility were realising the force
>> (i) of *Co-operation of Classes*, such as won Magna Carta, and carried Montfort on.
>> (ii) of *Individual leaders*—William the Marshal, Hubert de Burgh, Montfort—without a King's initiative, shaping National policy.
>> (iii) of *the spirit of Legalism*, which, in spite of Henry III's minority and folly, helped to sustain the system of Henry II, and fructified more fully under Edward I.

VII. Trouble with the **Scots** and **Welsh** under Edward I.

THE FRIARS. 1220—1400 c.

I. Revivalists at first :—finding Church lazy and apathetic,
Dominican monks preached self-sacrifice, and imbued many with enthusiasm for loftier ideals ;
Franciscans practised as social workers among the sick and wretched in *towns*.
Both professed Poverty, ∴ "*Mendicants*."

II. PHILOSOPHERS later
> (a) in **Theology** and **Physics** : famous at Oxford : e.g. Grosseteste, Bacon ; then their zeal for religion declined, and the **critical spirit** they awakened took a wider orbit ; hence
> (b) in **Politics**—they preached **democracy ;** King's responsibility ; the People (not only the Barons) should advise the King ; so they inspired Montfort.

III. *Religious Quacks* and *Impudent beggars* at last :—
> tried to attract charitable gifts : interfered with parish priests : granted absolutions cheaply : and on the whole supported the Pope :

∴ provoked the wrath of **Wycliffe** and **Lollards,*** and in 15th century ceased to be a force in politics.

PERIOD II 1272–1461.

Plantagenets and Lancastrians.

A. The **CONSTITUTIONAL STRUCTURE** rapidly advanced.

MONARCHY, set upon a *broader* basis by Edward I, becomes

I. More **Stable, Dignified,** in subjects' esteem;
∵ *All Britain* is brought under it;
Hereditary succession becomes the rule;
Lawyers' doctrines exalt its majesty;
Justice is more royally administered;
Military glories of Edward III, Henry V, yet

II. More **LIMITED** by the vigorous growth of **other organs** of the Body Politic:—

(a) *legislative, i.e.* **PARLIAMENT,** which takes the *Initiative in law making*:
invents *Privileges* for itself:
punishes, by *Impeachment*, evil ministers:
Deposes bad Kings, Edward II, Richard II.

(b) *executive, i.e.* **ROYAL COUNCIL,** which becomes masterful, *even over the King*:

(c) *judicial, i.e.* **COURTS,** which were forming that "Common Law"—the future touchstone of absolutist pretensions.

B. **POLITICAL POWER** is mainly with the **BARONS**;

∵ their *vast estates*, and numerous retainers:
the *War in France* braced and barbarised them:
their *connection with royalty* by marriages:
the *Church's* influence was *declining*:
their exceptional chances, when *Regencies* were required by King's absence, infancy, dotage;

∴ **I. Royalty**—they assail with *Oligarchic* schemes;

II. Parliament—they either *dominate* or *ignore*;

III. Royal Council—composed only of *leading Barons*, becomes the strongest organ in the State;

IV. Law Courts are thwarted by *Baronial licence:*
But the rivalry of Baronial clans for supreme power, coupled with the Dynastic question, issued in the

WAR OF THE ROSES; from which

THE CROWN emerges as **the strongest institution.** The *Constitutional machinery* survived, but was now to function only at the bidding of a *Despot*.

EDWARD I 1272—1307

The "**English Justinian**"
∴ (1) By *Legislation*
   he hoped to *consolidate* his realm.
(2) With *Lawyers* intimate, e.g. Burnell, Chr.
(3) Study of *Law*—he encouraged.

But he differed
∴ a great *warrior*: *not absolute*: co-operated with a national *Parliament*: was *hostile to* the *Church's* wealth: and the *Law* he nursed was *in its infancy*, whereas Justinian consolidated a system which had matured for 1,000 years.

The task he took in hand?

A. An EMPIRE OF BRITAIN—to consolidate : ∴ he subdued
(1) *Scotland*—temporarily ;
   and he meant it to send representatives to Parliament.
(2) *Wales*—for good ; he overcame Llewellyn and David ; and by **Statute of Wales** (at Rhuddlan) 1284 he created *5 new counties*, and established *Castles, Courts*, and *Sheriffs* on the English model.

B. GASCONY—to **retain,** against Philip of France.

C. THE MONARCHY—to **re-lay its foundations :**—
The shocks it had under Henry III warned him it must be limited *either* by a Feudal baronage, *or* by the Nation's co-operation ;

∴ **he re-settled the CROWN'S relations**

I. **To the PEOPLE :**—Rejecting a *feudal* basis for Kingship, he chose the broader support of *the People* ; so to them he secured

   (a) **Justice** more systematic :—

   He determined, for centuries, the development of our Private Law ∴

   (i) as an **Organiser**—he secured speedier Justice by *defining* the several Courts' jurisdictions ; and as "*Parliament,*" "*Council,*" "*Courts,*" were more clearly distinct, so ∴ were "*Statute,*" "*Ordinance,*" and "*Judge-made*" law.

   (ii) as a **Legislator**—he imposed a code * for the Courts' *uniform* guidance, thus advertising the Sovereign as supreme lawgiver ; v.i.

   (iii) as a **Patron of Lawyers**—he stimulated the growth of *English* Law as a home product, as a cult of *professional* laymen, detached from Ecclesiastics, and from the Roman Law.

- (b) **Representation** in a **National Assembly**:
    Montfort and the Friars had prepared the way;
    Edward wanted a counterpoise to Church and Barons, and a broader field for taxation;
    ∴ on the principle "*Quod omnes tangit ab omnibus approbetur*" he merged *land-tenure* in a *wider* qualification, and, drawing precedents from the *Great Council, Shire Courts,* and *Church Assemblies,* he called, on the eve of a campaign v. Scots,
    1295 a Model Parliament * of the 3 "**Estates.**"

II. **To the CHURCH**:—Hoping to fit it into his scheme of governments, he pared down some of its excesses;
    ∴ (i) Its *Courts'* jurisdiction was curtailed.
    (ii) Increase of its *wealth in land* was checked (1279).
    (iii) Some canons of *Convocation* he cancelled.
    (iv) He *taxed* it, and defied the bull "**Clericis laicos.**"
But to **lower** clergy he offered **representation** in Parliament.

III. **To the BARONS**:—These were proud of their fight with Henry III, and of Montfort's record, which had won them credit with the people:
    ∴ (a) Some by *marriage* were attached to the Crown, e.g. to Gilbert of Gloucester he gave princess Joan.
    (b) Others he *worried* with "**Quo Warranto**" **writ,** to make them justify in court their titles.
    (c) All had their *pre-eminence lowered* by
        (1) "**Distraint of Knighthood**":
            i.e. all landholders of £20 a year had to become Knights, or pay a fine.
        (2) "**Quia Emptores**" statute,* which multiplied Crown's tenants-in-chief.

But he met with some stubborn **opposition**
    from Earl **Warenne,** as to the "*Quo Warranto*" writ;
    from Earls **Bohun** and **Bigod,** who 1296 refused his demand for service in Gascony, while *he* went to Flanders.
This, coupled with the **Church's** anger at his taxes on it, and the **Merchants'** anger at his seizure of wool, led up to

1297 "CONFIRMATIO CARTARUM"
    i.e. of the Great Charter, and the Charter of the Forest;
    also—**No New Taxes,** without *Nation's* consent, to be levied by King, *except* old aids, prises, and wool duties.
This did *not* mention "*Talliages,*" ∴

1297 "DE TALLAGIO NON CONCEDENDO"—
    cited as a *statute* in Petition of Right; but it was probably only the Barons' *interpretation* of the C.C., not accepted by Edward, who levied a talliage 1304.

LEGISLATION of EDWARD I.

Mostly *without* concurrence of the *Commonalty,* by **STATUTES** of
Westminster I 1275
    Aids—for Knighting lord's eldest son, or dowering his eldest daughter, shall not exceed £1 per Knight's fee.
    Bail—unless X be in prison on charge of treason or murder, or by King's command, Sheriff to let X find sureties.
    Elections—shall be free.

Gloucester 1278
- (i) "*Quo Warranto*" writ—to make Barons justify, to the King's Judges, such franchises as e.g. their jurisdictions.
- (ii) "*Appeal of Felony*" for murder must be within 1 year 1 day.

Mortmain, i.e. "De Religiosis" 1279.
forbade transfer of *land* to *religious* bodies,
∴ King and Lords lost the feudal services.

Wales 1284 v.s.
brought Wales within the English system.

Westminster II 1285.
- (a) as to **Donum Conditionale** ("*de Donis*"), a gift of land to "*A and heirs of his body*" shall be a perpetual entail, *inalienable*.
- (b) "**Writ in Consimili Casu**"—to be issuable from Chancery for *cases analogous* to those covered by the *old, limited* writs.
- (c) **Commission of "Nisi Prius"**—legalised: i.e. for an issue of *fact* in a *Civil* case from e.g. Devon, ready for trial at Westminster, a Devon jury was to be sent up by e.g. May 1, *unless before* that date a Judge came on circuit to Devon. He *regularly did*.

Winchester 1285
- (1) Revived "*Assize of Arms*" 1181 v.s.; arms to be viewed twice a year by constables of hundreds.
- (2) "*Hue and Cry*" after felons: "*Watch and Ward*" in towns, were regulated.
- (3) *Highroads* to be free from trees for 200 yards on each side, lest robbers lurk there.

Westminster III 1290. "Quia Emptores":—
The grantee of a *fee simple* shall hold no longer of his grantor, but of the grantor's lord;
∴ (a) **Outright alienation** replaced *Subinfeudation*;
- (b) **Sub-Manors** were **no longer** creatable; for a "manor" needs at least 2 fee simple tenants.
- (c) Crown's **tenants-in-chief** were multiplied, ∴ the status lost in dignity.

"Articuli super Cartas" 1300
added to Magna Carta 20 clauses—e.g.
Limits to *Purveyance*, and to *Forest* jurisdiction:
Sheriff to be *electable* in *some* counties;
Exchequer shall *not* hear *common pleas*.

N.B. **COMPARISON of HENRY II and EDWARD I** shows them
ALIKE in I. Subjecting the **Church** in defiance of Pope:
II. Curbing the **Barons**:
III. Organising **Law courts**:
IV. **Securing the Commons** against local tyranny.

DIFFERENT in so far as **Edward** was
- (a) **Purely English** in sympathy; less engrossed with French possessions, he centred his aim on *consolidating Britain*.
- (b) **Broader** in **Legislative** scope.
- (c) **Less Absolute**; ∵ Magna Carta and Montfort's struggle lay between them; ∴ a livelier spirit of **Freedom** prevailed in *Towns*; ∴ *Commons* had got **Parliamentary representation.**

THE NATIONAL ASSEMBLY
Early history of PARLIAMENT?

I. **GREAT COUNCILS, non-representative,** existed prior to 1295

  A. **WITAN** (Saxon), concomitant to "**Personal**" Kingship.

    Aristocratic ∵ qualification was *Wisdom*.
    Activity manifold and real.
    Controlled King in theory; but he might "pack" it with thegns.

  B. **MAGNUM CONCILIUM** (Norman and Angevin)*
    Subordinate to **Feudal** sovereignty.
    Shrinks gradually to a "*Concilium Magnatum*":—

    (1) **Early Norman?**
      in *theory* = all landowners: met e.g. 1086;
      in *fact* = **Tenants by "barony"**;
        Bishops and King's **nominees**
        (∵ wisdom).
      Its power? in State trials, elections of Kings and bishops—*Real*; as to legislation and Taxes Illusory.

    (2) **Under Henry II?**
      more *Feudal*: **Tenants-in-chief,** major and minor, sat, but King could *limit* its size by *Special Writs*.
      more *Consulted* on legislation, alliances, war; but Taxes were practically as King decreed.

    (3) By **Magna Carta 1215** it was to be formed of **Greater** Barons and Church magnates by *Special* Writs; **Minor** barons—by *general* Writ, i.e. to Sheriff. *Its Consent* was to bind any barons absent, and to be vital to any *extra Aid* or *Scutage*.

II. **A PARLIAMENT** more **REPRESENTATIVE,**
    to co-operate with a **National King,** gradually took shape in the 13th century;
    ORIGIN of the HOUSE OF COMMONS?

A. PRECEDENTS for "REPRESENTATION"?
Known in old German politics, it had been adopted here for the formation
  (i) of **Church Councils**—to which the minor clergy of each diocese sent their "*Proctors*";
  (ii) of **Local Courts**—i.e. of Shire or Hundred; delegates attending from smaller units;
  (iii) of **Local Juries**—a few *Knights*, or "*legal*" men being elected
    to declare *information*, e.g. for "Doomsday";
    or to decide on *facts* in *judicial* dispute;
    or to *assess* payments, e.g. for the Saladin Tithe;
    or to *present* reputed *criminals*, then "Grand Jury";
  thus "**Representation**" was ready to hand for

B. ENLARGEMENT of our One-Chamber Assembly :—
  I. Circumstances contributing to this ?
    (a) *A counterpoise* was needed by the Crown, to Church and Barons, whose "Concilium Magnatum" was now too feudal and narrow to be national, or to be a safe foundation for the monarchy.
    (b) *A popular movement* towards democracy, stimulated by the Friars' teaching, was exploited by Montfort : v.s.
    (c) *A wider* field for direct *Taxation* was a royal necessity, and could be found in
      (i) the **Townsfolk,** now richer by Trade, and more independent by Charters;
      (ii) the **Knights,** now more numerous by absorption of minor barons, and busier with profitable farming.
    but (d) *Consent of the Taxed* was, by now, a *sine quà non* of direct Taxation; how was the King to get that consent ? Such commoners were too numerous to confer with him *en masse*;
      ∴ should send *Delegates* to speak for their respective *Communes*.

  II. Progressive Experiments in such "Representation" :—
  With the Magnates, were summoned
    in 1213 to St. Albans—*1 reeve and 4 men* from each Township;
      to Oxford—*4 Knights* . . . Shire.
    1254 *2 Knights* from each *Shire*, and *Proctors* for the clergy of each *diocese*.
    1265 to Montfort's Parliament :—
      with the Barons of his own party, *2 Knights* from each Shire; and to represent **Trade,** *2 elected* for each *City*, and each *Borough*.
    1295 to the "**MODEL" PARLIAMENT**
      of Edward I, embracing the *3 Estates*,
      (∴ all political constituents, either in person or by delegates).

(i) **NOBLES,** clerical and lay, by *individual* Writs.

(ii) to **represent** the **COMMONALTY**
- 2 Knights per Shire—by *writ to Sheriff*;
- 2 Citizens, 2 Burgesses—by *writ* for each *City* and *Borough*.

(iii) to **represent** the *lower* **CLERGY**—
as to each Diocese, by "*Præmunientes clause*" in the writ to each Bishop—

The *Dean,* and *Archdeacons,* to attend as such:
1 *Proctor* to represent *Cathedral* clergy,
2 *Proctors* to represent *Parochial* clergy.

But the above sat—each voting a separate "aid" to the King—as

(a) All the **Clergy** (spirituality),
(b) **Barons** and **Knights** (land),
(c) **Citizens** and **Burgesses** (trade).

C. THE FINAL SHAPE, i.e. **TWO HOUSES,** was not reached until 1330–40 :—

I. The **Lords*** : i.e. *Bishops, Abbots,* and *Lay Barons,* who attended not as delegates, but as a political Aristocracy, to **Advise** the King.

II. The **Commons :** i.e. *Knights, Citizens, Burgesses,* elected as *delegates* of their **Communes,** i.e. county, city, borough; and their function was primarily to **Consent to Taxes.**

The clerical "*Proctors*" soon deserted Parliament, and attended only "*Convocation.*"

THE "THREE ESTATES" of the realm:
How were they differentiated?

I. The **CLERGY** were drawn together by the Church's

(1) **Unity,** as an ancient, well organised, *Corporation*
(2) **Professional** status, and long monopoly of **learning.**
(3) **Privileges** in regard to
  (i) *Jurisdiction,* in Church Courts of Canon Law.
  (ii) *Self-taxation,* in Convocation, as to Church revenues.
  (iii) *Exemption,* from feudal dues, of their temporal wealth.

(4) **Landed Wealth** abnormal, which drew upon it
  (a) The Popes' studied regard; hence its habitual *deference to Rome,* which tended to *detach* it from the laity, and to place it almost *outside the body politic.*
  (b) The envy of Kings, Barons, and Social reformers; ∴ the fear of being "fleeced" in an assembly of *laymen* led the clerical proctors to desert Parliament.

II. The **NOBLES** became an order distinct,

> **Not** by **Caste,** as with the old French noblesse, whose numbers tended to increase, and whose privileges were invidious, e.g. exemption from taxes.
>
> **Not** by **Tenure** of a feudal Barony;
> though in fact most were great *landowners*, paid *feudal dues*, and retained a zest for *fighting*, when inferior classes were busy with Agriculture or Trade.
>
> **but** by their **Official relation** to the **Crown**:
> i.e. Church magnates and Greater Barons were marked off, because summoned to **advise** King in Council by *Individual Writs;*
>
> ∴ attended Parliament *personally*, not by delegates;
> ∴ a "**Political Aristocracy**" with
>
>> (1) Status *hereditary*, but devolving to eldest son only.
>> (2) *Tendency to die out*—corrected by Crown's new "*creations.*"
>> (3) *Privileges*, e.g. trial by peers, not oppressive to the commonalty.

III. The **COMMONALTY** became a coherent estate by

> (a) *Fusion* of Minor barons, **Knights,** simple Freeholders, who escaped military service, and stood for the *County* community, as a **Minor Landed Gentry.** And
>
> (b) *Association* of this order with the **Burgesses** of the *Town* communities;
>
>> ∴ (i) they had long *co-operated in Shire Courts*, when meeting Itinerant Judges, and electing Juries.
>> (ii) both represented the *growing National wealth*, to which Kings could look for subsidies.
>> (iii) all *too numerous* for King to invite them personally; ∴ by *general Writ to Sheriff* they were required to elect *delegates* for Parliament.
>> (iv) all conscious that these were sent for originally only to *assent to Taxes*: not to advise.

MEDIÆVAL PARLIAMENT

of 14th and 15th Centuries :

differed from the **Modern** as to

A. STRUCTURE and RAISON D'ÊTRE :—

> ∴ I. Not an **United Kingdom** parliament;
> (Scots, Welsh, Irish sent no M.P.s.)
> but was meant to reflect the 3 "**Estates,**" though
>
>> (a) In fact it tended to consist of *Landowners.*
>> (b) *Peers*, though fewer, were *stronger* than Commons.
>> (c) *Ecclesiastics* outnumbered the lay peers.

II. House of Commons was then **representative**
- (i) **Not** of **Individuals**: density of population was not, as now, the basis for distribution of seats; and several groups were unrepresented, viz.
  - *Lower Clergy*   *Landless freemen*
  - *Minor Townsfolk*   *Villeins.*
- but (ii) of **Communities**: i.e. from each of about 37 *Counties*, and 100 *Boroughs*, whatever their size, 2 M.P.'s were sent; and the county M.P.'s i.e. the Knights, led the voting.

B. PRIDE OF POSITION :—little appreciated then was the *right* to send M.P.'s, or the *honour* of sitting as M.P. ∵ local affairs were more engrossing, and travelling was risky and expensive.

C. CAPACITY and ACTIVITY ∵

- **Then**—It *sat* only for about *1 month* a year; usually was *led by the Barons*; a more coherent, *independent* body ∵ often at *variance with a King* who personally ruled : ∴ busy mainly with his demands for **Taxes,** and with criticism of the **Administration.**
- **Now**—Commons have nearly a *monopoly of power*; but too dominated by the spirit of *Party*, and split by *Faction*, to act independently. It is rather a machine worked by the Ministry, who bid for the Electorate's support with schemes of **Legislation.**

EDWARD III 1327—1377.

Patron of Art and Commerce : brilliant in Warfare : but unscrupulous as to his Promises, and hopeless in Finance.

A. REGENCY of 14 Barons ; but **MORTIMER** and **ISABELLA** domineered 3 years.

  I. **Mortimer**, with the boy-King, failed against the Scots ;
  ∴ made the *Treaty of Northampton* 1328.

  II. **Edward** trapped Mortimer (with Isabella) at Nottingham ; the peers found him guilty ; ∴ he was executed as a Traitor 1330.
  Later Edward, by **marriages,** attached to the Crown great *Baronial families* ; result of this is seen in the next reign and in Wars of Roses.*

B. SCOTS * still gave **trouble,** supported usually by France.

C. HUNDRED YEARS' WAR v. France * started **1338,** ended **1453.**

D. BLACK DEATH 1348 :—a Plague, destroying half the population ;

E. PARLIAMENT'S energetic **GROWTH** favoured by King's long absences and need of funds ; and by the *harmony of Lords and Commons.*

  ∴ I. Further **LIMITS ON THE MONARCHY** :—

  (i) as to **War** and **Peace** Parliament was consulted ; it was asked to approve e.g. treaties of *Northampton* and *Bretigny*.

  (ii) **Purveyance** to be subject to instant payment 1362.

  (iii) **Initiative in legislation** was secured 1354 ∵ the Commons' *Petitions* were to become laws by King's assent.

  (iv) **Taxation at will** was further denied to the King : 1362 No special tax on *Wool* unless Parliament assents.
  1373 "*Tunnage* and *Poundage*" * were created by Parliament.

  (v) **Appropriation,** of money voted, to *the War,* occurs 1353.

  (vi) **Conditional Grants** of subsidies for the War ; i.e. Redress of *Grievances* was made the condition of *Supply* ;
    in **1340** on condition that **Talliages** were abolished.
      1341 when Edward returned and, angry at emptiness of treasury, attacked Abp. **Stratford,** who claimed *trial by peers,* Parliament again voted money on **Conditions.**

II. **LEGISLATIVE MEASURES** on matters of **National interest** :—

Labour question—**Statute of Labourers** 1351
stopped "Free labourers" being "sturdy beggars" ∴ it compelled work at wages of *2 years before Plague*.

Papal Influence—**Statute of Provisors** 1351 ;
to stop Pope giving English benefices to Italian priestlings, usually absentees.

Statute of Præmunire 1353 ;
∴ Penal to uphold, against the King, Papal authority here, e.g. by *Bulls*.

Judges' discretion—**Statute of Treasons** 1352 * limited this crime to 7 forms.

Trade—**Statute of the Staple** 1355 ;
to simplify collection of export duties, *wool, cloth, leather, tin, lead*, to be sold only in 16 towns ;
∴ "*Merchants of the Staple*" became a privileged association, better able to bargain with foreigners.

III. Lively **CRITICISM OF THE ADMINISTRATION**
esp. on the **loss of** nearly all **Aquitaine** 1371–1376.

(a) An **Anti-clerical party**, backed by **John of Gaunt**, blamed *Churchmen* holding *State offices* esp. chancellor Wykeham, and the treasurer Bishop of Exeter. ∴ King replaced these with *laymen* Thorpe and Scrope ;

∴ **John of Gaunt** became **paramount**, but proved a failure ;

∴ (b) **GOOD PARLIAMENT 1376,**
led by Peter de la Mare (Speaker) and Wykeham, attacked John of Gaunt's party : and

(1) **IMPEACHMENT** * was invented against *Latimer, Lyons,* and others, for financial frauds ; they were cashiered and imprisoned.

(2) **Petitions** were addressed to the King
for *Annual Sessions.*
Free Election of the Knights.
A Council of 9 to be named by Parliament.

But **John of Gaunt** was enabled, by the King's dotage, to usurp *royal prerogatives*. He reversed the doings of the "Good" Parliament, e.g. pardoned Latimer, etc. ; and made a bid for **Popular Support** by joining in the cries of **WYCLIFFE AND LOLLARDS,*** "*Down with Popery,*" "*Plunder the Church*" ; but his supremacy ended with Edward's death.

THE HUNDRED YEARS' WAR
1338—1453.

CAUSES? Philip wanted Aquitaine: tampered with its nobles: and backed the Scots against us: Normans plied piracy on our coast.

Edward III resented *homage* to Philip: *claimed French crown* (through his mother) to draw *Flanders* to his side; and took into his pay *Lewis of Bavaria*, and *German Dukes*.

Stages of the War?

A. VICTORIES for us at first :—

(1) Sluys 1340: **Crecy** 1346: Calais taken 1347. **Truce 8 years.**

(2) Black Prince triumphed in Languedoc; and at **Poictiers** 1356 captured King John. France then torn by anarchy, ∴ was glad to conclude

(3) **Peace of Bretigny 1360** :— ∴ **Truce 9 years**, and Edward to resign claim to French crown; but to keep Aquitaine as a *free* duchy.

[**Black Prince,** to win Spain's help in Aquitaine, helped **Pedro** to regain Castile; unpaid by Pedro, he had to levy a hearth-tax on Gascony, whose barons appealed to French King, ∴]

B. War renewed—**DISASTROUS for us**—1369–1375.

Henry of Trastamara, Pedro's brother and foe, defeated our fleet; John of Gaunt made a futile march through France; all **Aquitaine was lost** to us, except Bayonne and Bordeaux.

[**Richard II 1393** made a **25 years' Truce**]

C. BRILLIANT REVIVAL 1411—1420 by HENRY V ;

∴ France was afflicted with a lunatic King, Charles VI, and the strife of *Burgundians* v. *Armagnacs and the Dauphin*; ∴ would have " bought off " Henry, who asked too much ;

∴ (a) **Agincourt 1415,** won by Henry, who then conquered Normandy and northern France, and was joined by the Burgundians, whose duke John was murdered by Armagnacs 1419.

(b) **Treaty of Troyes 1420** : Henry to be *Regent* of France at once, and *King* on death of Charles.

D. INGLORIOUS END under **HENRY VI** :—

I. **Duke of Bedford,** as Regent in France, mastered the north; then besieges Orleans; but

(i) **Joan of Arc 1429** relieved Orleans, defeated **us at** *Patay*, and re-kindled French patriotism ;

∴ (ii) Burgundians 1435 quit our side, and are reconciled to Armagnacs. Paris fell. Bedford dies.

II. Richard of York was successful, with Talbot, in Normandy; but, through Lancastrian jealousy, was recalled 1444;

∴ **III. Somerset** took his place; but, he being an incompetent general, and Henry VI favouring peace,

∴ **Truce of Tours 1446,** negotiated by Suffolk;
We to cede our fortresses in Maine and Anjou;
Henry to marry Margaret of Anjou.

but **IV.** *France renewed* the war 1449
Normandy (but not Calais) was lost by Somerset's fault; Bayonne and Bordeaux finally fell, when Talbot was defeated and slain at **Castillon 1453.**

EFFECTS of the **Hundred Years' War** on **English politics?**

I. The THRONE of **Edward III** and **Henry V** was **steadied** by our victories; Kings who were heroes of war had little to fear from Barons. But

(a) *Need of war funds* placed Edward at Parliament's mercy.*
(b) Policy required *peace with the Scots.*
(c) Of the *French wives*, yielded by the truces to Richard II, Henry V, Henry VI, the last, Margaret of Anjou, proved to be a curse to England.

II. The BARONS found a wide **field for their energies**; home politics were the calmer for their absence.

But (a) Their appetite for **plunder** was whetted.
(b) Their **prestige** was lowered in the nation's eyes.
∴ (i) Feudal fighting tactics were discredited in the war; battles were won by *dismounted knights*, and *yeoman archers.*
(ii) As leaders, they failed conspicuously in the final campaigns.
∴ all the readier to seek plunder and military renown in the **Wars of Roses.***

III. PARLIAMENT—more **unanimous** in the absence of the King and the fighting barons—became
(i) **Progressive,** in voting money on *its own terms*;
(ii) **Critical,** in searching for scapegoats, when the war went against us; N.B. On the loss of Aquitaine 1374, the *anti-clerical* movement.*

IV. The PEOPLE were **exasperated** by the
(1) **Heavy taxation**; N.B. The **Peasants' Revolt** 1381.
(2) **Final loss** of Normandy, Bayonne, Bordeaux; hence *Suffolk* was impeached 1450.
Somerset was dislodged from power.
Cade's Rebellion 1450* which advertised, and gave a lead to, **Richard of York** in the Wars of the Roses.

THE CHURCH in the 14th century.

It was declining in influence, and estranged from the laity, which it no longer helped to political liberty;

∴ **(1) Personally** it had *deteriorated*;
after the Plague many unfit were ordained;
and it no longer monopolised learning.

(2) **Papal Control** robbed it of a *National* character.

(3) **Church Courts** were oppressive; and, as they applied *Canon Law*, stood outside the *Common Law*.

(4) **Bishops** and **Abbots** were intent on politics, theology, or profits of land. Papal dogmas served for articles of faith.

(5) So **Wealthy**—yet exempt from ordinary taxation; hence luxury and apathy *within* the Church, and the envy of Socialists *without*.

A REACTIONARY MOVEMENT was thus provoked: hence

A. National, patriotic, attitude of **Parliament**:—
Popes then being the tools of our enemy France,
∴ Statutes of *Provisors* * and *Præmunire*.*

B. Anti-Clerical spirit, which animated
  (i) John of Gaunt's friends, who would drive Churchmen from *State offices*; and confiscate Church wealth.
  (ii) Peasant Revolt, 1381.

C. Heresy and **Socialism** of **THE LOLLARDS,**
who exaggerated in practice what was taught (1368–1384) by **WYCLIFFE**, a master of Balliol. This movement was

  I. Religious ∴ he *challenged the Pope's* authority: denied *transubstantiation*, and the need of a *mediating priesthood*; and

  II. Socialistic ∴ the Villein revolt was backed by the Lollards; and Church's wealth denounced, so that
    (a) *Taxation* might be fairly distributed;
this to win sympathy from Lancaster's faction;
    (b) *Clergy* by poverty might be *spiritualised*;
this the motive preferred by Wycliffe.

Lollards were strong at first e.g. in Oxford, and tolerated by Richard II and his wife Anne; but their teaching became **revolutionary** (e.g. that laws unscriptural could be defied); they formed **conspiracies,** e.g. *Cobham's 1413*; some were burnt; so their influence

  (a) In *politics* came to *nothing*;
∴ Want of a good leader.
Villeins' grievances were removed.
Lancastrian Kings' devotion to the Church.

but **(b)** In *religion* endured as a *Protestant spirit*, and prepared England for the **Reformation.***

FOURTEENTH CENTURY:
Its constitutional interest?

The Monarchy, left strong by Edw: I, was yet **confirmed**
- (a) by the **Hereditary** sequence of the 4 Plantagenets, Edwards I, II, III, and Richard II.
- (b) by **Lawyers' theories**—dignifying Kingship—
    - (i) "*King never dies*," i.e. King's death will not suspend the reign of Law.
    - (ii) "*King can do no wrong*," ∴ responsibility for misrule must be fixed not on King personally, but on his Ministers.

The KING'S COUNCIL * was growing distinct and powerful, **co-ordinate** in some degree
- (i) with *Parliament*, ∵ for some statutes its Assent is recited; and it could make "*Ordinances*" without consulting the Commons.
- (ii) with *King himself*, as in Richard II's case.

But, in **resistance** to such expansion of Royal power,

A. REVOLUTIONARY efforts by groups of **BARONS** (when King was a weakling, dotard, minor, or tyrant) tending to **OLIGARCHY**—rule by a few magnates with motives mainly selfish—and either
- (i) Ignoring the Commons: see **Lords Ordainers 1311**;
- or (ii) Impressing Parliament's support:
    - see **John of Gaunt's party 1375** * ; **Lords Appellant 1389**.

B. Steady Growth of a CONSTITUTIONAL POLICY:
- **I. Structure** of Parliament was completed about 1340, 2 separate Houses: fusion of Knights and Burgesses.
- **II. The Commons gained** in relation to the Lords, and the **Crown,**
    - ∵ (a) their *Concurrence* in legislation was made necessary, and the "Ordinances" annulled for want of it, 1322.
    - (b) their *Petitions* could shape a Statute, 1354.
    - ∴ (c) they maintained "*Grievances shall precede Supply*."
    - yet, when without the Barons' leadership, they yielded to the autocrat Richard II.
- **III. Parliament as a whole** advanced in power and activity (see Edw: III). It asserted a claim
    - (i) To *appoint Ministers and Councillors*, but this was occasional, and later given up.
    - (ii) To *Privilege*, e.g. in Stratford's case.
    - (iii) To control *Taxation* * (see Edw: III)
    - (iv) To hold *Ministers Responsible*, as when
        - 1327 Stapledon and Baldock were punished as ex-ministers of Edward II.
        - 1376 Latimer, etc., were **Impeached.**
        - 1386 Suffolk was **Impeached.**

HENRY IV 1399—1413

first of the Lancastrians : son of John of Gaunt.

A. THRONE INSECURE at first ∴ his **TITLE** rested

Not on **Hereditary** right : the boy *Edmund Mortimer* had this, by descent from Lionel of Clarence, an elder brother of John of Gaunt.

but on **Parliament's choice**—the Church, and a faction of Barons, having hoisted him, to serve their own schemes.

∴ **no hearty loyalty** from the mass of his subjects ; and he had to cope with

I. REBELLIONS and WAR from his declared OPPONENTS—

(a) **Avengers of Richard II**
  (i) Earls of Kent, Salisbury, Huntingdon revolted ; ∴ Henry had Richard starved to death.
  (ii) French King (Richard's father-in-law) planned invasion, and aided Welsh rebels.

(b) **Champions of Edmund Mortimer**
  i.e. *Mowbray* and *Abp. Scrope* revolted in the north but were suppressed by *Neville*, and both were executed without due trial.

(c) **Patriots** of **Wales** and **Scotland** ;
  a blow for independence being struck by
  (i) *Welsh*—under *Owen Glendower*, aided by France, and he was hardly subdued by the end of the reign.
  (ii) *Scots*—under *Douglas* ; defeated by " Hotspur " at *Homildon Hill 1402*. Henry demanded the Scot prisoners from Earl Percy, who refused ; ∴

(d) **The Percies** rose in **feudal defiance** ;
  but were defeated at *Shrewsbury 1403*, and again at *Bramham Moor 1408*.

II. HIS SUPPORTERS' demands for " CONSIDERATION " :

(i) His **Baronial** party had to be kept in good humour, but his *poverty* made this difficult, ∴ he lost the Percies over the Scot prisoners' ransoms.

(ii) The **Church**—∴ Abp. Arundel required persecution of Lollards ; ∴ the statute **de Heretico Comburendo 1401.**

(iii) **Parliament**—though it obliged him with this statute, in other ways made him " toe the line " ∴

B. PARLIAMENT—especially the **COMMONS**—

strengthened itself, at the Crown's expense, by way of

(1) Interfering with the King's Council ;

1403 He removed certain Ministers *by its request*.

1404 He chose, *at the Commons' request*, a **Continual Council of 22** (Bishops, Lords, and Commoners).

1406 Petition of " **31 Articles** " :—that he should *nominate* 16 Councillors : they to *swear* to respect Common Law : no office in Treasury, Chancery, or Household to be held for *life* : King's *revenue* to be spent on King's household or debts.

(2) **Finance**
1400 "*Grievances to precede Supply*" was pressed on him.
1404 *Account* and *Audit* of his expenditure was demanded. Royal demesnes not to be aliened.
1407 **Money Bills** must *originate* in the **Commons.**

(3) **Privilege** of Parliament
(a) In *Impeachments*, only the Lords are to be Judges.
(b) *Freedom of Speech* was vindicated as to *Haxey M.P.* and King must *not notice* discussions in Parliament.
(c) *Freedom from Arrest*, in so far as an assault on M.P. was penalised 1404.
(d) In *disputed Elections*, Sheriffs' returns were to be scrutinised in Parliament 1403.

Yet

C. He **LEFT** Lancastrian throne fairly **SECURE** ∴

I. By his **military energy,** supplemented by his **crimes,** he had suppressed the various Revolts.

II. By **lucky chances** he was enabled to meet
(a) danger from the *Scots*:—∴ he captured their prince James; so he kept the Scots' Regent Albany quiet, by threat to restore James.
(b) danger from *France*:—∴ there the strife of factions enabled him to weaken each, by joining first Burgundians, then Armagnacs.

III. By the **popularity** and military **genius of his son,** Henry of Monmouth, the nation became reconciled to the new dynasty.

WARS OF THE ROSES 1455—1485.

I. **ORIGINATED** in
a **dynastic question**—was the **legitimate King** *Richard of York*, with title hereditary by descent from Lionel of Clarence, an elder son of Edward III ?
or *Henry VI*, whose title was no better than Henry IV's, i.e. parliamentary ∴ John of Gaunt had been a younger son of Edw : III ?
pointed by the **political misrule** of Margaret, Suffolk, Somerset, and Henry's incompetence.
and **splitting** the **Barons,** who were closely allied with royalty, as the result of Edward III's "family policy."

∴ II. **INFLAMED** by the **blood feuds** of Baronial clans, now fewer and richer, and intent on plunder, and on recovering prestige lost in French war ;
Yorkists were esp. *Mortimers, Nevilles, Mowbrays.*
Lancastrians were esp. *Beauforts, Percies, Talbots, Courtenays.*

III. **ENDED** (when many of the barons were killed off) in a **Personal Quarrel** between
King **Edward IV** and Kingmaker **Warwick.**
Usurper **Richard III** and Avenger **Henry of Richmond.**

RESULTS of the WARS OF THE ROSES?

A. OLD BARONAGE was DESTROYED ;
∴ (1) **House of Lords** lost stability and independence.
(2) **Feudal households** were broken up: arable land was turned into pasture, ∴ many were out of work ; hence *economic* discontent.

B. MIDDLE CLASSES
in *Commerce*—were but little affected.
in *Social status*—gained by the ruin of Feudalism.
in *Politics*—lost their leaders, ∴ **Parliament** was soon **overborne by King** and **Council.**

∴ **C. CROWN was left immensely STRONGER ;**
traditional checks on it fell into abeyance ; the machinery of Constitutional government remained, almost complete in form, but there was no one to work it.
∴ a "**New Monarchy**" begins with **Yorkists and Tudors :—**

I. *Richer* by the vast confiscations, and forced levies from traders and yeomen ;
∴ **Parliament** could be **neglected.**

II. *Relieved of opposition* from old baronage, it created, and leaned on, a **New Nobility,** which reinforced the **Council.**

III. The *People, tired* of the anarchy of Civil war, now rated **Security** above political liberty, ∴ **ready to tolerate the firm despotism of the Tudors.**

CURIA REGIS — ROYAL or PRIVY COUNCIL.

Its development until 1461.

A. *Dependent on an Absolute King*
(whose privilege, not duty, it was to call a Court of consultants, confidants and agents) was the Norman "**Curia Regis**" a term used of

I. **GREAT COUNCIL** * i.e. magnates and tenants-in-chief ; met occasionally, and was sometimes merged with

II. **CONCILIUM ORDINARIUM**—a permanent body of **Officials** of State and Household, and a few magnates ;

(a) **Functions** as manifold as King's own powers, *financial* : *legislative*, e.g. shaping "Assizes" : *judicial*, for appeals and tenants-in-chief.
∴ as business increased, it

(b) **Delegated**, under Hen: I, Hen: II, special work to definite Committees :—
(i) *Exchequer* for financial Account, Receipt, and later Jurisdiction.
(ii) *Judicial Committee of 18*, reduced 1178 to 5 Judges = "**King's Bench**" = **Curia Regis (III)**

Yet **C. Ordinarium,** parent of so many offshoots, retained a paramount *Jurisdiction* ; **also,** in a less purely official form, became, **by the minority of Henry III.**

B. *More Independent*—as a *political* Council of King's **PERSONAL ADVISERS**

    (1) **Necessary** as a complement of the *Limited Monarchy*, which reformers had in view.

    (2) **Separated** more from the Great Council and Courts under Edw : I, who ruled it, and exacted *Oath of Secrecy*.

    (3) **Responsible,** in as much as " *King could do no wrong* "
    ∴ he could be checked only through his ministers ;
    ∴ a long struggle began for

C. *Control over Council* by **(a) Barons ; (b) Parliament** :

   I. Methods of checking this **EXECUTIVE ?**

    (a) *Election*, by Barons, of chief Officials, e.g. Justiciar, Treasurer, 1258, 1311 ; but a strong King resented this : e.g. Edw : III 1341.

    (b) *Oath* required from each Councillor, e.g. to respect Common Law, to take no gifts.

    (c) *Statutes* by Parliament (Edw : III) against Council encroaching on Common Law by " *Ordinances*."

    (d) *Salaries* fixed by Parliament 1406.

    (e) *Impeachment*,* e.g. 1376, 1388 ; but this was suitable only for the gravest misconduct.

    (f) *Nomination* by Parliament of *All* the Council under Hen : IV, Hen : V, and Hen : VI till 1437.

   Most of these were ineffectual ; and, though much of the *work* of the old Curia Regis had passed to Parliament, Chancery, Treasury, Common Law Courts, yet **by the early Lancastrian period**

   II. PRIVY COUNCIL'S power became **Immense :**—*though* **subordinate to Parliament** by appointment, *yet*, ∵ minority of Ric : II, weakness of Hen : IV, absence of Hen : V, minority and weakness of Hen : VI, it was at least **co-ordinate with the Crown.** Composed of **about 12 Barons and Bishops**—its activity was

    (i) *Executive* ∴ a Regency with sovereign powers :

    (ii) *Legislative* ∵ by its " *Ordinances* " it could encroach on Common Law, and relax Statutes.

    (iii) *Financial* ∴ it could raise Loans on State credit ; regulate staple Trade ; control Aliens.

    (iv) *Judicial*—for Appeals and Baronial offenders ; and it could summon anyone to appear.

   But **from 1437** King appointed to the Council ; ∴ Parliament's influence over it waned ; ∴ it became, **by middle of 15th century**

D. *Uncontrolled Organ of Government ;*
identified with the Court party 1450 c, it failed to check Baronial lawlessness, to secure common justice ; ∴ after the War of the Roses * it became the **obedient instrument of Despotism** under the Yorkists, Tudors, first 2 Stuarts (the " *Age of Councils* " *)

FIFTEENTH CENTURY:
Its CONSTITUTIONAL INTEREST?

I. *In the First half*—Lancastrian **King's dependence** enabled **PARLIAMENT**

  A. *To retain ground won in 14th century:*

    ∴ still Conditional grants of money:
- Appropriation of Supply, e.g. 1404.
- Scrutiny of Accounts.
- Impeachment, e.g. of Suffolk.

  B. *To extend its growth* by way of

    I. CONTROLLING the **EXECUTIVE** ∴

    Privy Council was appointed by Parliament; cf. the "*31 Articles.*"

    Not King, but Parliament, shall nominate the Regents and Protectors 1422.

    II. Perfecting its **PROCEDURE** and **PRIVILEGES**:—

    ∴ (i) *Money Bills* to originate in the Commons.
    (ii) In *Impeachment* the Lords to be judges.
    (iii) *M.P.s'* freedom of Speech (*Haxey's* case) freedom from Arrest (*Thorpe's* case) were vindicated; and King was not to notice discussions in Parliament.
    (iv) *Sheriffs' returns* to be revised in Parliament.
    (v) *Bills*, not Petitions, to introduce Statutes.*

II. *In the Latter half*—a **retrograde tendency,**
    ending in a **New Monarchy** of Yorkists and Tudors. See "Results of Wars of the Roses." *

PERIOD III 1461–1603.
Yorkists and Tudors.

PREROGATIVE RULE, veiled with Legality,
practically unchallenged until Elizabeth's reign;
Constitutional advance and **Political liberty** are held up.

A. This "NEW MONARCHY," though
limited in theory, was

I. ABSOLUTE in fact—governing **personally**, with **no check** from *Church, Parliament, Baronage,* or *Bench*:

by agency of great **Commoners**, and **Privy Council** Committees,

behind a **veil of legality**: i.e. **Church, Judges,** or **Parliament** were used to sanction despotism.

II. POPULAR with the nation—because of

its pageantry: its tactful regard for public opinion: its **great services** in *Education, Commerce,* and *championing* England against the Pope and Spain.

III. ULTRA-PATERNAL—as the period advanced: e.g. Elizabeth's interference with personal religion: thus provoking a sharp **REACTION,** ∴

B. The NATION was OUTGROWING
Paternal rule.

FORCES were gathering—from the "*New Learning,*" the *Reformation, Commercial expansion,* and the *Conflict with Spain,*—which were to burst such restrictions, and carry forward a **Constitutional Movement next century.**

These, broadly described, were

I. The spirit of SELF-ASSERTION:

men by now were *thinking for themselves*;
∴ challenged (a) dogmas of the *Church*:
(b) fiats of royal *Prerogative*.

The **Puritans** embodied this independent spirit;
∴ they led the **Reaction.**

II. The sentiment of NATIONALITY, intensified

by our closer contact with European diplomacy;
by our breach with Rome;
by our Conflict with Spain:

England, more isolated, was ∴ more conscious of her distinction as an **Independent State;** hence her great impatience of those Stuarts, who courted *Spain,* or sold themselves to *France.*

WHY WAS TUDOR MONARCHY SO STRONG?

I. **Wars of Roses** * resulted in a New Monarchy, in which constitutional forms were used to *disguise*, not to restrain, *despotism*.

II. **England's condition** needed a strong **Personal Rule**;
∵ (a) *Foreign dangers*: ∴ *diplomacy* became all important, a game played better by Kings than by Parliaments.
 (b) *Conspiracies* were bred by doubts as to the Succession; ∴ need of a detective eye, and summary methods.
 (c) *Trade* prospered, ∴ a desire for peace and order.
 (d) *Strife of Creeds*, ∴ need of an arbiter to prescribe a middle course.

III. **Papal Supremacy**, which Hen: VIII took over, supplied precedents for arbitrary rule, e.g. *Dispensing power*.

IV. **Popularity** of the Tudors: due to their
 (i) Strong *individuality*.
 (ii) Respect for *public opinion*.
 (iii) *Court pageantry*, which advertised the Crown's majesty, and gratified National pride, livelier since our recent introduction to European politics.

V. **People** were too **uneducated** for self-government, **diverted** from politics by commerce and new learning, and now **without leaders** to organise opposition;
∵ (a) *Old Nobility* was weakened by the civil war, and swamped by new peerage.
 (b) *Church* had lost the nation's confidence, turned to the King for support, and was by Hen: VIII subjected to the Crown.

VI. **Parliament weak**, and, till Elizabeth, **Servile**:
Peers, ∵ mainly new creations; bishops were the King's nominees; abbots and priors ceased to attend.
Commons, ∵ those who might have led them were made peers; elections were influenced; new boroughs created.

VII. **Faithfully served** by
 (a) *Upstarts* raised to office, e.g. Empson, Dudley, Wolsey, Cromwell, Cranmer, Gardiner, Parker, Cecil.
 (b) *Privy Council* * and its various committees, esp. Star Chamber,* superseding Parliament and the Courts.
 (c) *Judges* obsequious, holding office at King's pleasure.

VIII. **Despotism** was **veiled** by an outward observance of *Legality*; esp. Hen: VIII tried to get a *legal sanction*
from the Church for his divorce:
from Judges for e.g. benevolences.
from Parliament for most of his tyranny.*

LIMITS TO ROYAL POWER under the TUDORS ?

I. *In theory and fact* **Monarchy** was **limited** in that Parliament's assent was needed for (a) Direct Taxes.
(b) New Statutes.

II. *In theory*, though not in effect,

(a) **Ministers** were responsible : **yet** *no Impeachments*.

(b) **Judges** were sworn to heed no royal mandates : **yet** they gave the *replies King desired*.

(c) **No man** could be arrested without a warrant, or convicted without a jury : **yet** n.b. *Star Chamber*.

(d) **No indirect taxes** were imposable by Crown, **yet** e.g. "*Monopolies*" were known.

III. *In fact* the **main Restraints** were :—

A. Want of a **Standing Army.**

B. Want of **Funds**—compelled Hen : VIII and Elizabeth to appeal to Parliament, not always successfully.

C. Uncertainty as to the **Succession,** ∴ **Plots**
(1) by *impostors*, e.g. Simnel, Warbeck ; or
(2) in support of *possible successors*—Buckingham, Pole : Northumberland's, Wyatt's : and Mary Queen of Scots.

D. Foreign or **Papal Influences** inciting
(i) *Schemes* of impostors under Hen : VII.
(ii) *Aggressions* of the Scots.
(iii) *League* of Catholic Powers against us.
(iv) *Plots* to dethrone Elizabeth.

E. Public Opinion at home ; Tudors studied, and often deferred to, this ; they had to reckon with

(a) *Independence*, born of middle-class prosperity ; more than once Commons resisted even Wolsey.

(b) *Critical spirit*, awakened by New Learning ; some theories now on politics, e.g. by More.

(c) *Conservative sentiment* of
(1) Lower Orders, regretting the monasteries.
(2) Old Nobility, hating the new officials.
(3) Catholics, resenting royal supremacy.

(d) *Non-conformist* conscience of Puritans.*

HENRY VII 1485—1509.

What favoured his chances of Despotism?
 I. *Crown* was *stronger* after Wars of the Roses.*
 II. *Devoted Service* of middle-class men.
 III. *Power of the Purse*—he fully realised and used.
 IV. *New Artillery* monopolised by Crown ;
  ∴ rebels were more easily quelled.
 V. *Spain* and *France* were examples of firm Absolutism.

DIFFICULTIES HE HAD TO MEET?
 A. HIS TITLE to the throne—**Not Hereditary ;**
  ∵ descended, by father, from the widow of Henry V :
   by mother, from a *prenuptial* son of John of Gaunt (legitimised 1397, but barred from Crown)
  ∴ *inferior to Yorkist* issue of Edward IV, and of Clarence ;
   but (1) he was to *marry* Elizabeth, daughter of Edw : IV ;
   (2) as victor of Bosworth he *possessed* the throne ;
  ∴ **Parliament declared** the Crown to vest in **him and his heirs.**

 B. REBELLIONS by **Yorkist** pretenders and malcontents.
  I. by **Lovel** 1486 in the north, where Yorkist sentiment was strong ; he was promptly suppressed.
  II. by **Lambert Simnel** 1487 ; an Oxford carpenter's son, who personated *Warwick* (Clarence's son). Crowned in Ireland : encouraged in Flanders by Margaret (Edw : IV's sister) : defeated at Stoke, Lovel and earl of Lincoln being slain.
  III. by **Perkin Warbeck** 1491-99 : a Fleming who posed as *Richard* (Edw : IV's son) ; started in Ireland : received in France and Scotland, and in Flanders was *supported* warmly *by Margaret* and *Philip* ; ∴ **Henry**
   (a) Cut off our wool trade with Flanders.
   (b) Executed Warbeck's friends here, e.g. Stanley.
   (c) Passed "**Act for security of service** to a *de facto* King" = *that service even to a usurper, even martial law in rebellion or invasion, shall not be punishable, even by Parliament, in a later reign,* 1495 (cited as a plea for the Regicides 1661).
  Warbeck was later **repudiated**
   (i) by Flanders : ∴ "*Intercursus Magnus,*" i.e. free trade with Flanders, arranged with Philip.
   (ii) by Scotland : then he landed in Cornwall, attacked Exeter, was captured in New Forest. In the Tower he plotted with Warwick, ∴ both were executed 1499.

IV. by **Cornishmen,** under **Flammock** 1497, who resisted a subsidy for war with Scots; crushed by the King's *artillery* at Blackheath.

C. Our WEAK HOLD on **Ireland, Scotland,** and esteem of **Europe**: impostors ∴ easily got outside support;

∴ **I. Poyning's Act** 1494: existing English laws were to bind Ireland, and her Parliament was not to legislate without leave of King and Council. *Repealed 1783.*

II. Alliance of Henry **with Ferdinand** of Spain, by whose aid
    (a) he tried in vain to prevent France absorbing Brittany;
    (b) he diverted the enmity of *Margaret, Philip,* and *Scotland*; so the way was paved for

III. Marriages, diplomatic and lucrative, arranged between his son *Arthur* and *Catharine* of Aragon.
    daughter *Margaret* and *James IV* of Scotland.
    daughter *Mary* and *Charles* of Austria.
    and *he* proposed *himself* for *Margaret of Burgundy and others*.

D. LAWLESS remnant of the OLD BARONAGE:
whose "*Livery*," "*Maintenance*," "*Rioting*" baulked the course of Justice, and supplied pretenders with bands of adventurers;
    ∴ **a strong Central control** was **needed**;

∴ (a) **Judges** and **Sheriffs** were directly admonished by the King to enforce the laws.
    (b) **Privy Council** was recruited from middle classes; from *clerics*, e.g. Morton: from *lawyers*, e.g. Empson, Dudley.
    (c) "**Star Chamber Act**" **1487** * revested in 7 Councillors and Judges the criminal jurisdiction of Curia Regis, to stop Maintenance, Livery, and Rioting by Barons too mighty for the ordinary Courts.

E. POVERTY, which had **crippled Lancastrian Kings**:—
∴ he **amassed Wealth**—not by general taxation, but
by (1) *Benevolences* and *Forced Loans* from the rich.
    (2) *Forfeitures* of Yorkist rebels' estates.
    (3) *Fines* for offences, under even obsolete statutes.
    (4) *Feudal dues*—exacted with extreme rigour.
    (5) *Bribes*, e.g. from France under Treaty of Etaples.

Thus he was **independent of Parliament,** which he called only 7 times, and *discontinued nearly 13 years.*

HENRY VIII 1509—1547.

HIS FOREIGN POLICY ?

A. Against France he joined *Spain and Pope*, hoping to recover the French duchies ;

but (1) Scots were aggressive, ∴ were defeated at *Flodden* 1513.

(2) Wolsey's diplomacy aimed at avoiding war, by balancing France against Spain : ∴

B. Peace with France 1514 ;

but *Charles* of Spain became "Emperor" 1519.

Wolsey kept Charles and Francis hoping for English support, and sought Charles' aid to win the papacy.

Henry was still anxious to win back French duchies.

∴ **C. Against France he allied with Charles 1521 ;**

but I. *Charles* proved a selfish ally : money ran short : Scots gave trouble : ∴ Henry was tiring of Charles, until

II. *Charles* at **Pavia** 1525 defeated Francis ;

then *Henry* proposed a joint invasion of France ; but *Charles*

(i) Gave no return for Henry's money.
(ii) Schemed to keep Henry and Francis apart.
(iii) Played Wolsey false over the papacy ∴

D. Peace with France 1525, arranged by **Wolsey :—**

Henry to get 2 million crowns, and peace with the Scots.

Alliance with France 1527

∵ Charles was growing over mighty ; and the Divorce case further estranged him (Catharine's nephew) from Henry.

But I. *Charles and Francis came to terms* 1529

∴ Pope Clement was encouraged to refuse the Divorce ; Henry vented his rage on Wolsey, who died in disgrace.

II. *Henry's Reformation work was completed* by 1537 ;

then (a) **Pope** tried to combine Charles and Francis against Henry ; ∴ Cromwell tried to league England with German Protestant States ;

(b) **James V,** hostile to Reformation, sided with Pope, and married Mary of Guise ; thence a sinister influence was active in France ;

∴ (c) **Francis** aided the Scots ; would not pay Henry his debts ; and *broke with Charles* by siding with Turks.

∴ E. **Against Francis**—Henry **allied with Charles 1543**: and captured Boulogne. But Charles played false, and made terms with Francis; and Scots gave trouble ∴.

F. **Peace with Francis 1546;**
Henry to have 2 million crowns: Boulogne to be the security.

THE REFORMATION
1529—1536.

(i) a **Legal** and **Political** movement by **Henry VIII,** who established his **Supremacy over Church** by
fining the *Clergy* for the "*præmunire*" of recognising Wolsey's Papal commission to correct abuses in the Church here:
limiting *Convocation's* powers:
assuming the nomination of *new Bishops*:
diverting *Annates* from Pope to the Crown:
stopping *Appeals* to Rome:
obtaining from (1) Clergy, (2) Parliament
 a *Recognition of his supremacy*:
dissolving *Monasteries*, and seizing their *wealth*.

(ii) **Not until** Edward VI and Elizabeth were **Liturgy** and **Doctrine** fully reformed:
N.B. **Henry VIII** had written against Luther "*Assertio septem sacramentorum*," ∴ "*Fidei defensor*"; and 1539 affirmed the **Six Articles** of Romanism; yet allowed translation of Bible, and parts of the Liturgy.

HOW far was the REFORMATION ANTICIPATED?
By

A. **KINGS' previous attitude** towards Church and Pope :—
William I, e.g. as to Convocation's canons.*
Henry I and **John,** as to Bishops' appointment.*
Henry II, as to Church jurisdiction, and Appeals to Rome; cf. "*Constitutions of Clarendon.*" *
Edward I, as to Taxation of Clergy, and Mortmain law.*
Henry VII, restricting "Benefit of Clergy."

B. **PARLIAMENTARY Measures :—**
(1) *Provisors'* statute 1351, as to Papal *patronage*.*
(2) *Præmunire* statutes, as to Papal *jurisdiction*.*
(3) *Anticlerical policy*, led by John of Gaunt 1371.*
(4) *Alien Priories'* wealth, *confiscated* to Henry V.

C. **POPULAR MOVEMENTS of protest**—led by
 (a) **Hubert de Burgh,*** against Money payments to Rome.
 (b) **Wicliffe** and **Lollards,*** against Catholic doctrines, Papal authority, and Church's wealth.
 (c) Colet, Erasmus, More, Tyndale, Latimer—**liberal thinkers** and **preachers,** hostile to dogmatic religion.

HOW was the REFORMATION EFFECTED?
1529—1536.

By a series of **Statutes**—passed in a servile Parliament, on **T. Cromwell's** initiative :—

A.— REFORM of Ecclesiastical ABUSES :—

(1) Clergy *trading, pluralities, non-residence,* prohibited 1529.

(2) Church *Courts'* procedure was *restricted* 1532, i.e.
No excessive probate fees.
No citing of a person outside his diocese.
No *Benefit of clergy* for any inferior to subdeacon.

B. CHURCH to be LEGALLY SUBJECT to the SOVEREIGN :

∴ I. **Convocation's** legislative power was curtailed, i.e. No *Canons* to be valid without King's assent; this by Convocation's "*Submission*" 1532: and by "*Act of Submission of the Clergy*" 1534.

II. **Election** of a **Bishop**, by the Chapter, to be only by "*congé d'élire*" from King, and of King's nominee; this by "*Annates Bill*" 1534.

III. **Monastic Wealth** was diverted to Crown 1536, 1539; it was vested in a "*Court of Augmentations.*"

C. POPE'S SUPREMACY over Church was TRANSFERRED to KING :—

∴ (a) **Appeals to Rome** were **prohibited**

as to *marriages, wills, oblations* 1533 ;
Absolutely 1534, by "*Act for Submission of Clergy.*"

N.B. *Act of Succession 1534* declared Catharine's marriage void, Anne Boleyn's valid, and settled crown on her issue; acceptance of the Act was required on Oath.

(b) **Annates**, and other payments to Pope, **to cease ;** and a new bishop needs no papal confirmation. this by *Annates Bill 1534*

(c) **Even** in matters **Spiritual**—King to be **Supreme :**

(i) admitted by *Convocation* 1531 "*So far as Christ's Law allows,*" when the Clergy, charged with "præmunire" for recognising Wolsey's papal authority, submitted, and paid £120,000 for pardon.

(ii) declared absolutely by "*Act of Supremacy*" *1535,* giving King power to correct *heresies* and *abuses*; an *Oath of Supremacy* was required; to refuse it was treason. Cranmer held that the King, as *a channel of divine grace,* might even consecrate a bishop.

EFFECTS OF THE REFORMATION?

A. CLERGY lost independence

  I. In *political* standing

  ∴ now mere servants of the Crown: could no longer balance Pope against King, lead an opposition to tyranny, or command a majority in House of Lords. Prelates tend to be Court sycophants, not premier statesmen.

  II. In *spiritual* control

  ∴ now that **Religion** was "**an affair of Statute,**" they had no claim to authority but by King's leave; they lost the prestige of connection with Rome, and were expected to preach under royal inspiration.

B. CROWN gained

  ∴ now champion of Church against heresy within, and the Pope without: active supremacy in religion made civil despotism more feasible.

  But this re-union of Church and State bred **Nonconformity**; *religious* differences by persecution became *political*;

  ∴ (a) **Catholics** imperilled the throne of Elizabeth *
  (b) **Puritans** * ultimately upset the Stuarts.

C. NOBILITY—now **a new order,** creatures of the Crown, richly endowed with monastic lands;

  ∴ (1) Bound by interest to resist a revival of popery;
  (2) Dominant in House of Lords—a pillar of the throne;
  (3) Dealing with land in a *commercial spirit*, they provoked *revolts*,* by rejecting the old style of farming.

D. ENGLAND as a whole was

  In foreign relations now **isolated,** at variance with the Catholic Powers, and exposed to a Spanish invasion until after 1588: hence arose **a National spirit.**

  Internally, moved towards **political** and **personal Liberty;**

  ∴ (a) The *strife of creeds* generated a heat in which Parliament resumed vitality;
  (b) The *fall of Papal authority* awoke—especially in the middle classes—a **critical, reforming spirit,** which was soon to question even the authority of the Crown.
  (c) *Subjection* of even the *Church* to the *Law* confirmed the **Spirit of Legalism.**

ELIZABETH 1558—1603.

MAIN OBJECTS OF HER POLICY?

A. To preserve UNION of STATE with REFORMED CHURCH :—
Temporal authority to be supreme over *Spiritual*;

∴ **I. To define** the established **Religion,** and insist on **Conformity,** *without the Crown championing either extremity of doctrine.*

II. To sustain **Tudor Prerogative**; hence a **Despotism**
 (a) *Ecclesiastical*—challenged by Papists and by Puritans, though on different grounds.
 (b) *Civil*—challenged, but not fiercely, by an awakening House of Commons.

B. To GUARD THE THRONE and ENGLAND'S INDEPENDENCE
 against political bondage to Spain
 religious bondage to Rome.
Danger threatened from

I. Mary Stuart's claim
which, being likely to aid, was aided by, the

II. Ambitions of Foreign Powers—
Pope—served by Jesuits and seminary priests.
France—the Guises intriguing for control of Scotland.
Spain—whose Philip stirred Irish revolts, and designed, by the Armada, to annex England.

∴ **III. Plots,** numerous on behalf of Mary Stuart,
 unmasked by the vigilant Burleigh and Walsingham.

C. To secure INTERNAL PEACE and ORDER :—
 ∴ (1) To stop agrarian discontent and vagrancy
 ∴ she established a new **Poor Law.**
 (2) To settle Ireland, which was torn by the Revolts of O'Neill 1561 : of Desmond 1579 : of Tyrone 1598.

D. To promote TRADE, and **cure** the nation's **bankruptcy :**
 ∴ she inspired *maritime enterprise*, encouraged *colonisation*, and conferred *charters* e.g. on the East India Company 1600; but prosperity was felt only in towns, not in rural districts.

FOREIGN POLICY of ELIZABETH.

A. HOSTILE, at first, **TO THE FRENCH,** who dominated Scotland, and hoped, through Mary, to absorb England.

∴ **I. To win over the Scots**—she aided Scot Protestants against the regent, Mary of Guise : held out marriage to earl of Arran : crushed the French forces ; then had her title as queen of England recognised by *Treaty of Edinburgh* 1560.

II. **To secure Spain's neutrality**—she played on Philip's fear of France, and held out marriage to his relative, Charles of Austria.

III. **To keep France paralysed** with religious strife—she allied with the *Huguenots* v. *the Guise* (Catholic) *faction*.

B. **SPAIN and the POPE** soon became **the greater FOES :**

∴ (a) **Netherlands' Revolt** v. Spain 1568, and Duke of Alva's atrocities to the Dutch, brought closer to us the Spanish peril ;

∴ (i) She *helped the Dutch*—though meagrely—with money, and told Hawkins to catch the Spanish treasure-ship.

but (ii) She *refused sovereignty* (1575) of Holland and Zealand ; ∵ she wished Netherlands to be a buffer State, taking off from us the shock of Spanish aggression.

Our trade benefited by the influx of Dutch merchants and French craftsmen, but Puritanism here was recruited by these continental Protestants.

(b) **Bull of Pius V,** " deposing " Elizabeth,
encouraged *Plots* to which Spain was privy.

(c) **Mary Stuart**—as the Guise influence waned in France—appealed to **Philip of Spain,** to help her to win the English throne.

∴ I. Elizabeth *tried to balance* France against Spain ;
∴ held out marriage to Duc d'Anjou, brother of the French king Charles IX, with whom she made an Alliance.

II. 1572 *St. Bartholomew Massacre* (of Huguenots) strained that alliance, but she sent no active aid to Huguenots.

C. **The ANTI-PROTESTANT LEAGUE** in Europe **1576 ;**
by the **Pope** and **Spain,** working through Jesuits, and, in France, the **Guises ;** opposed by Henry of Navarre: created difficulties for Elizabeth ∴

I. In **Ireland,** Desmond's revolt : In **Scotland,** Esmé Stuart's Plot.

II. In **England** Jesuits were preaching treason, and had to be ruthlessly exterminated.

III. In **Netherlands**—Don John, Alva's successor, meant to coerce the Dutch, marry Mary Stuart, and invade us ;

∴ 1580 when the lower Netherlands chose *Duc d' Alençon* as protector, Elizabeth held out marriage to him, to prevent France joining Spain ; he died 1583.

but 1584 *William of Orange*, Protestant prince of Holland and Zealand, was *murdered* by a fanatic Papist.

∴ 1585 *She openly allied with the Dutch*, and sent Leicester with troops enough to sustain their struggle.

IV. In **France** 1585, Henry III was persuaded, by the Guises and Philip of Spain, to veto all Protestant worship.

∴ D. **OUR BREACH WITH SPAIN** was now **nearly complete** :—

What circumstances led up to the ARMADA ?

I. **PHILIP** stood for **a type of Despotism,** civil and religious, abhorrent to most Catholic, and all Protestant, English, who remembered the

  (i) *Marian persecutions* to which he was privy :
  (ii) Atrocious *tyranny* of his deputies *over the Dutch* :
  (iii) *Plots* against Elizabeth's throne and life :
  (iv) Spanish monopoly of *colonial trade* :
  (v) *Inquisition*, which had tortured English sailors.

II. **ELIZABETH'S** England, already **free** from the bonds of **Rome,** was nearly in sight of **political** liberty ; and she had exasperated Philip by

  (a) *Refusing* his offer of *marriage* 1559.
  (b) *Aiding the Dutch* with money and men.
  (c) *Raids* on Spanish traders by our "sea-dogs," and seizure of the treasure destined for Alva.
  (d) *Massacre of Spaniards* by Raleigh in Ireland.
  (e) *Persecution* of Catholics, especially Jesuits, and dismissal of the Spanish ambassadors.
  (f) *Execution of Mary Stuart*, who had assigned to Philip her claim to the English crown.

So **Philip**—now relieved of pressure
  from Netherlands—since murder of William of Orange ;
  from France—by the war of religions there—
was ready to claim England *in his own right* ;
  hence the "**Armada.**"

E. **AFTER the Armada**

  (1) *Against Spain*—still an aggressive policy, favoured by the younger party, e.g. Essex sacked Cadiz.

but (2) *To Henry IV* of France—help was sent under Essex when Catholics there urged Philip to come and conquer ; Henry became a Catholic 1593, thus re-uniting France ; still he, Elizabeth, and the Dutch, held together.

ELIZABETH'S **RELATIONS WITH PARLIAMENT.**

A. **She was dictatorial :** it sat for only 22 months in her reign.

Not rich enough to dispense with it, she packed it by creating new boroughs, influenced elections, and controlled the Speaker. It addressed her in loyal terms, and, while the State was in peril, did not press hard for reforms ; but

B. **The Commons awoke** from their long apathy :—

  ∴ (i) *Education* had advanced since Henry VIII :
  (ii) *Independence*, born of middle-class wealth :
  (iii) *Sense of perils* threatening the State :
  (iv) Heat of *religious strife*, **Puritan M.P.'s** being loudest in protest ; ∴ collisions with the Queen as to

I. **PRIVILEGE of free DEBATE** on " matters of State " ;
"*your privilege is Aye or No*"; i.e. no *initiative* for Parliament :

∴ (a) As to her **Marriage** and the **Succession** :—
She vetoed discussion, though both Houses prayed her to marry, or name her successor ; ∴ speeches in protest, by Paul Wentworth 1566, Peter Wentworth 1593.

(b) As to **Church Reform** :—a matter, she said, not for Parliament, but her *Prerogative*.

∴ 1571 *Strickland*, for his Bills, was dismissed from Parliament ; but, on protest, she forgave him.

1587 *Cope's " Bill & Book "* (for a new Prayer Book) ; she coerced the Speaker : Peter Wentworth protested : he and Cope were imprisoned.

1593 *Morice*, for his Bill to reform the Church Courts, was imprisoned.

II. **PRIVILEGE of scrutinising ELECTIONS** of M.P.'s.
County of Norfolk case 1586 :—as to issue of a Writ for a 2nd election, the queen said it lay with the Chancellor and Judges ; but the Commons appointed a committee, which held the first election good.

III. **Attainder of Mary Stuart?**
After Ridolphi's plot, Parliament wished to proceed thus ; but Elizabeth refused to assent.

IV. **MONOPOLIES** 1597—1601
She had granted to courtiers exclusive rights of trading, in e.g. salt, leather, glass ; ∴ prices were inflated. Parliament, *bolder now that the State was out of danger*, petitioned against them. She long demurred, but finally assented to their abolition by **Act of Monopolies** 1601.

ECCLESIASTICAL POLICY of
ELIZABETH, as compared with Henry VIII's.

A. **HER CLAIM** was *not, as Henry's was*, to be a **channel of grace**, consecrator of bishops : but to be **" GOVERNOR "** of religion, with indefinite *disciplinary power* ;
∴ her reversal of Mary's changes began with

ACT OF SUPREMACY 1559

(1) Crown to have all Spiritual **jurisdiction,** and **corrective power ;** to assert the Pope had it—on third offence—was treason.

(2) **Oaths** of Supremacy and Allegiance to be required from all clerics and crown officials.

(3) **Commissioners** to be creatable by her, to exercise this prerogative. (∴ *High Commission Court 1583*, v.i.).

Unlike Henry—she resented Parliament dealing with Church reforms ; and bishops, who refused the oath, were only deprived, not executed.

B. **PROTESTANT LITURGY** and **DOCTRINE** were re-imposed :—
   Henry made no such change; but Elizabeth, though herself favouring ornate ritual, yet, to allay the strife of Romanists and Calvinists, took a **via media** which should satisfy moderate men, e.g. *clergy to be celibate*; but *no " Mass "* :

   1559 **ACT OF UNIFORMITY**
   Imposed a revised **Prayer Book :** penal, if a minister deviated from it : absence from Church to be finable.

   1563 **Thirty-nine Articles** replaced the 42 ;
   but not obligatory on clergy till 1571.

   1565 **Parker's " Advertisements "**
   —to warn Puritans :
   a guidance as to *discipline* and *ritual*.

C. **HER INTERFERENCE** with **Personal Religion ?**

   I. **Tolerant** treatment *at first* **of Nonconformity,**
   (a) *While it was consistent with loyalty ;*
   ∴ she professed to be content with *outward* conformity, leaving Opinion free. Most Catholics did thus conform.

   but, (b) *After Pius' Bull* 1570, Popery meant Treason; plots were numerous ; State perils, such as never confronted Henry, provoked

   II. **Persecutions**—fortified by Statutes—
   (a) of *Papists*, ∴ fanatical papists imperilled the throne; ∴ suffered, not for their *religion*, but for their *treason*.

   (b) of *Puritans*, ∴ they challenged her prerogative of Church *discipline*, offended her taste and *sense of order*, and threatened the Church's organic *unity*, the maintenance of which was so vital in the struggle with Rome.

CIVIL DESPOTISM of ELIZABETH

Can be *accounted for*—if not *warranted*—

I. As the complement of her **ecclesiastical Supremacy** (so greatly emphasised ∴ so keenly challenged), though not—as *that* was—legalised by Parliament.

II. By **State Perils**—at a period when a standing army was unknown here, the loyalty of many was suspected, and Burleigh was ever on the watch for a plot.

III. By **Precedents** of Henry VII, Henry VIII, and Mary—who **practised** extreme " Prerogative," and were not so ready as Elizabeth to gracefully yield on protest.

IV. By a Theory, then held, that the **"Prerogative,"**
>though (i) Mainly *Limited* and *subject to Law*—
>>so wrote Hooker and Sir T. Smith:
>
>yet (ii) Partly was *Absolute* and *paramount to Law*, so far as necessary for the State's safety; thus spoke her courtiers. But no " plea of *Necessity* " can be urged for most of
>>**HER ARBITRARY RULE,** as illustrated in the

A. Proclamations, creating new offences;
e.g. even *rioting* was made capital; and by
Star Chamber Ordinance 1585 the Press was gagged.

B. Imprisonments, by the fiat of any Privy Councillor, often in places so remote that *Habeas Corpus writ* was defeated; this provoked a protest from Judges.

C. Patents, issued to courtiers, e.g. for trade *Monopolies*, or for *exemption* from process for debt.

D. Trials unjustly conducted ∴
>**I.** *In arbitrary Courts*
>>**Star Chamber *—High Commission Court *—Court Martial ;** e.g. 1595 some London apprentices for brawling were thus tried and executed.

or **II.** *By illegal Procedure*—for **political** offences :
>i.e. juries were packed : torture used : judges acted as prosecutors : men were convicted on scanty evidence; e.g. *Udal* and *Penry*, for the " marprelate " tracts; and *Stubbe* lost his hand for deprecating the match with Duc d'Alençon.

E. Opposition she showed **to** Parliamentary **Privilege * :** She coerced the Speaker; forbade discussion on matters of State; imprisoned M.P.s for obnoxious bills.

THE SUCCESS of ELIZABETH'S
REIGN—How far due to the QUEEN ?

The **MAIN PURPOSES *** were **her own ;** Burleigh was a vigilant sentinel, not a constructive statesman.

The **MEANS** and **METHODS** adopted may be ascribed

A. Partly to the **QUEEN'S CHARACTER :—**
>**I. Mistress** of the art of choosing **good servants,** and urging them to strenuous effort, she never had to sacrifice them to popular rage; yet she was slow in gratitude, and slow to spend.
>
>**II. Autocratic**—especially in *resenting Parliament's* interference with *matters of State.**
>
>**III. Unsentimental**—∴ though vain and pleasure-loving, her caprice as a *woman* easily yielded to her policy as a *queen*, e.g. her abstention from marriage, and the execution of Essex ; "*religious* " she was, but only from *political* motives ;
>Yet **sympathetic with her people,** and beyond an empire in their hearts her ambition never ranged.

IV. Loving Order and **Discipline**—hence her severity to the Puritans, and street brawlers.

V. Temporiser—fond of a balanced position; hence the "*via media*" she took in Religion; her *finesse* and *vacillation* in diplomacy; waiting to take advantage of her foes' mistakes, she made it her aim to keep them in troubled waters.

B. **Chiefly** to the **zeal** of her **MINISTERS** and **SERVANTS,** partly inspired by bigotry, or by the spirit of the age.

To **Burleigh** and **Walsingham** we may ascribe:

(i) Alliance with Huguenot leaders;
(ii) Detection of Plots, and measures for the queen's safety;
(iii) Removal of Mary Stuart;
(iv) Persecution of Catholics.

To Abp. **Parker**—the Church Discipline and Articles.
To Abp. **Whitgift**—the High Commission Court's oppression of Puritans.
To **Drake, Howard, Hawkins, Raleigh**—the harrying of Spain, and the daring enterprise which helped the nation, caught unready, to overcome the invader.

With the *literary brilliance* of her reign neither queen nor minister can be credited: that was the lustre which naturally gathers on an age of stress and heroism.

ADVANTAGES OF TUDOR RULE
to England of 16TH CENTURY?

I. EDUCATIONAL ∵
(a) New **Schools** and **Colleges** were founded
(b) The revolt from Rome, following the intellectual awakening of the **Renaissance,** led men to think for themselves; *dogma ceased to satisfy*: **liberty of Opinion** is asserted on religious, social, and political questions.

II. ECONOMIC ∵
(1) **New modes of culture** were applied to the redistributed monastic lands: *then* a grievance—*later* found *profitable*.
(2) **Trade** gained by *peace* and *security*, by influx of *alien craftsmen*, by *exploration*, and *colonisation*.

III. POLITICAL ∵
A. **National Spirit** was roused by resistance to the Pope, the triumph over Spain, and England's improved status abroad.

B. **Royalty** was **popularised** ∵
(i) *Crown*, in touch with *Nation's pulse*, identified itself with its subjects' interests.
(ii) *Loyalty* became a matter of *religion*, when the Crown championed the national creed.
(iii) Amid grave external perils, *paternal guidance* was supplied to a nation just growing up.

C. **Strong Central Government,** by Star Chamber and other Councils ;
      ∴ (a) *Security* replaced 15th century Lawlessness.
      (b) *Old Baronage ceased to be oppressive*; the day of great commoners had arrived.
      (c) *Middle classes* became buoyant, and independent.
      (d) *Ireland, Wales,* and *the North,* were drawn closer.
   D. **Local Government** was recast :—
      Parishes became administrative units : *Poor Relief* was started : *Justices* of the Peace got wider functions.
   E. **Constitutional Machinery**—just because it served the King's will—was preserved in **good order.**
      Parliament increased in size, and was by Henry VIII charged with such *sovereign functions* (e.g. changing Religion, fixing the Succession) that in the 17th century it awoke, and *realised* its capacity to **share sovereignty with King.**

HOW DID TUDOR POLICY LEAD UP TO PARLIAMENT'S STRUGGLE WITH STUARTS?

   A. Tudors were absolute in fact—governing
      (i) in **Religion**—by assumption of the Pope's powers; by aid of *Bishops* and *High Commission Court*; Mary and Elizabeth trying, by *persecutions*, to school their subjects into obedience.
      (ii) in **Politics**—by strong Councils (esp. *Star Chamber*), docile Parliament, pliable ministers; depressing the old nobility, raising the middle classes : with a liberal use of
         (a) **Proclamations** * : (b) **Arbitrary taxation** :
         (c) **Martial Law.***

But B. *The People were stirred by two new forces* :—
      (1) a **National spirit**—after the conflict with Rome and Spain; this was fostered by the Crown.
      (2) a **Critical, individualistic, spirit**—stimulated by the new education, study of the classics, and Bible-reading; and embodied in the **Puritan party.** Now that Papal authority was impugned, what institutions could go unchallenged ?

and C. *Parliament,* under Crown's guidance, *did sovereign acts*; was increased by nearly 200; learnt to act together, and so became conscious of strength, claiming "**Privileges.**"

∴ **At the STUART accession,** the conditions of the coming storm were nearly complete :—
   I. The **KING—JAMES I**—expected to inherit the Tudors' powers : found for them a *theological* basis, and relied on **Bishops** and **upstart favourites ; Star Chamber** and **High Commission Court** became deadly weapons of tyranny.

II. The **NATION** now was too **self-conscious** to be *argued* into passive obedience; needing a sympathetic leader, it resented a tactless, intolerant, pedantic autocrat.

III. The **PARLIAMENT**, reflecting both the **national** and the **self-assertive spirit**, claims a share in **sovereignty**, and **privileges** *independent of the King's grace*; strongly reinforced, as it was, by
   (a) **Lawyers,** well **educated,** the brain of the Commons, who championed the **Common Law** as against *Chancery, Church Courts,* and unlimited "*Prerogative.*"
   (b) **Puritans**—who, after their sufferings under Elizabeth, expected from the *Scotsman* sympathy, but got oppression; who stood for **liberty of thought,** and lent to the *legal* and *political* struggle the passion of *religious* zeal.

THE STAR CHAMBER
1487—1641.

A. *Originated* **CONSTITUTIONALLY**
   as a Court of **Criminal Equity,** to meet the occasion, un-tied by legal precedents, and backed by the supreme **Executive's** might;

∴ I. **PRIVY COUNCIL** ever had a vague **reserve of jurisdiction** (specialised already for *civil* matters in the "*Chancery*").
   (a) *exercised* in a room in Westminster Palace, where the ceiling was starred, or where Jewish bonds (Starra) were filed;
   (b) *resented* by Parliament when it encroached on the Common Law Courts; but *favoured* in so far as it relieved their rigidity, or supplemented their inability to cope with overmighty subjects in disorderly times.

∴ II. **1487 STATUTE** of "**Livery** and **Maintenance**" ("*Star Chamber Act*"), declared a quorum of *Seven* of the Council were to deal with certain **crimes against** public **Order,** and course of **Justice,** viz. *Maintenance, Riot, Bribery of jurors,* and *Sheriffs' official misconduct.*

B. *Enlarged* **POLITICALLY,** in pursuance of Wolsey's policy,
   as to **Personnel**—for *any* of the Council might sit in it; but later the Court *localised* at Westminster became distinct from the Council *attendant on the King.*
   as to **Functions**—for its jurisdiction extended to a variety of
      (a) **Crimes**—i.e. if **misdemeanours** of **public** import, e.g. *Sedition, Conspiracy*; and to its control of Printing we trace the origin of our law of *Criminal Libel,* as a menace to *peace.*
      (b) **Civil cases**—e.g. if parties were *Corporations,* or *Aliens*; but not those referable to Admiralty, Chancery, or Court of Requests.

Thus, **while the period of disorder lasted,** the Court was popular, its work salutary; ∴ it was commended by Sir T. Smith (temp. Elizabeth) for "*bridling stout noblemen*"; and called by Coke "*The most honourable Court*" in Christendom.

But, **when Tudors had secured peace and order,** it lost its old *raison d'être,* and hardens into an excrescence, *impeding constitutional growth,* ∴

I. SERVIENT merely to ROYAL CAPRICE :

no longer a court of *Judges* protective of peace, but a clique of *Politicians* enforcing the *King's policy,* e.g. stifling the Press, or worrying Puritans ;

II. OUSTING the authority of PARLIAMENT :

∴ it could legislate by "*Ordinance*" or "*Proclamation,*" and execute its own decrees *irresponsibly* ;

III. UNCONSTITUTIONAL in its PROCEDURE :

for this violated *Common Law traditions,* ∴
No jury : not usually a trial by equals :
Self-convicting answers were extorted : Torture was adopted. And, though it could not *directly* sentence to death, *it punished Juries* which acquitted in a *capital political* case,
e.g. Throgmorton's 1555.

It thus became, under Jac : I, Car : I, **INCONSISTENT** with the Demand for **Restrictions on Prerogative :**
Reviving **Authority of Parliament :**
Dignity of **Common Law,** asserted by Lawyers ;

∴ After its unscrupulous activities against the Crown's Puritan critics (e.g. *Prynne* 1637, for his "*Histriomastix*") —it was **abolished** by the **Long Parliament 1641,** *as having exceeded the authority vested in it by the 1487 Statute.*

THE COURT OF HIGH COMMISSION.

Mary commissioned certain Churchmen to investigate *heresy* ;

A. **Elizabeth**—finding several bishops unreliable—by **ACT OF SUPREMACY** 1559 got a power to create a Court paramount over the Bishops' Courts, ∴ *welcomed by their enemies, the Common Lawyers.* Hence there were issued

I. Against PAPISTS, at first, temporary commissions to

tender the *Oath,* enforce *Conformity,* and exercise **the Queen's jurisdiction over the Church.**

II. Against PURITANS, 1583, a PERMANENT COURT, by

advice of Whitgift, to enforce the **Liturgy** and vindicate the **unity of the Church.** 44 members, mostly laymen ; but a quorum was 3 ; one of these, and the chief, to be *Bishop.*

Its **scope?** An "*Inquisition*" as to heresy, schism, contempts, seditious books, immoralities ; but it could not inflict torture or death.

Its **procedure**? By "*Oath ex officio*," i.e. a series of questions framed so as to trap the accused into a self-convicting answer.

Thus Puritan clerics *and laymen* were harassed: hatred of episcopal rule increased: the "**Mar-prelate**" **tracts** were provoked: *Puritans* were aggravated into a *political* faction.

B. **James I** and **Charles I** strongly encouraged the Court, to vindicate the **dignity of Bishops** and "**popish innovations.**"

But (i) *Lawyers*, e.g. Coke, now disputed its right to fine or imprison the *laity*.

(ii) *Laud, Abp.*, so mercilessly abused its powers against the King's opponents, as to contribute largely to the causes of the Civil War;

∴ Abolished by the Long Parliament 1641, with all other ecclesiastical jurisdictions; nor was it revived, with these, in 1661; but

C. **James II** revived it in 1686—to re-introduce Popery—as the "*Court of Ecclesiastical Commission.*"

∴ **Bill of Rights** 1689 finally declared any such Court to be **Illegal** and **pernicious.**"

PERIOD IV 1603-1688.
The first four Stuarts.

PREROGATIVE RULE, in contempt of the Law, provoked the **STRUGGLE of the 17th CENTURY** for Political Liberty and English Protestantism.

Battle cries:—Supplied by *Institutions*, whose place and power in the Constitution were challenged:—" **Kingship,**" " **Parliament,**" " **Church,**" " **Bench,**" " **Army.**"

Dramatic episodes:—Great **Rebellion**: **Cromwell's Policy**: **Execution** of one King: **Expulsion** of another: **The Great Revolution 1688.**

A. THE KING'S PARTY stood for

ABSOLUTISM religious and secular;
modelled on the Spanish or French type;
warranted **BY " DIVINE RIGHT ";**

∴ I. **PREROGATIVE,** in State affairs, to be **above Law;**

II. **COUNCILS,** e.g. Star Chamber, nominated and inspired by the King, to execute **his will;**

III. **BISHOPS** and **JUDGES** to be his **servile** tools.
Such a creed would be *fatal to Political Liberty*; ∴

B. THE POPULAR PARTY marshalled,
against it, **forces** which had been gathering for over a century:—

I. The **CONSTITUTIONAL** spirit—which deprecated irresponsible Kingship, and demanded a balancing of powers as between *King* and *Parliament*.

II. The **LEGAL** spirit of the English—which expects *Judges* to be *independent*, and the Ordinary " *Common Law* " to prevail, *without exceptions*.

III. The **RELIGIOUS** zeal of Protestantism—which fired
Puritans—to an uncompromising *self-assertion*, over royal dictation as to personal religion;
Anglicans—to a resolute *opposition*, when James II tried to restore Romanism.

IV. The **NATIONAL** spirit—which could not tolerate a King who aped the Spaniard, or sold himself to France, involving, as this did,
(a) the menace of **Popery;**
(b) the **loss of** England's **independence.**

THE REVOLUTION of 1688 finally affirmed the victory of English **Protestantism** over *Popery* from France; **Parliament's** sovereignty over rule by "*Prerogative*."

THE STUART DESPOTISM
in contrast with the TUDOR :—

A. NOT REQUIRED by England's position, ∴
  (1) *Strong* now abroad, *orderly* at home; no serious plots, as under Elizabeth, threatening the throne.
  (2) The *Nation*, now more *educated*, was ready for some *self-government*; this national spirit, fostered by the Tudors, was thwarted and wounded by the Stuarts.

B. MORE PERSONAL and DIRECT tyranny by the King :
  e.g. James' quarrel with Coke : Charles' invasion of the House of Commons; whereas **Tudor** *tyranny* appeared to proceed from the Crown's **ministers** and **delegates** ; ∴

C. NOT POPULAR, i.e. not based on a **concord** of **King and People** ;
  James I and Charles I did not expect, or court, popularity, but relied on a circle of *Bishops, Courtiers*, and servile *Judges*; and, whereas Tudors were satisfied with absolutism *in fact*, Stuarts laboured to give *reasons* for it—the **theories** that
    i. By "**Divine Right**" King is irresponsible, a god upon earth ; Bishops were vital for teaching the people this doctrine : ∴ "*no bishop—no King.*"
  or ii. **Prerogative,** as to matters of **State, is independent of all law :** thus spoke the servile **Judges.**
  or iii. By an **Original Contract,** between all subjects, the King was invested with omnipotence, a being who is *outside the "body Politic"* : thus wrote **Hobbes** 1651.

∴ **D. DISDAINED the LEGAL FORMS of the Constitution ;**
  ∴ a tyranny over *institutions*, not merely over individuals : e.g. Parliament was Henry VIII's favourite tool ; but the Stuarts resented Parliament's co-operation : they showed *no anxiety to have tyranny legalised.*

∴ **E. PROVOKED a more EDUCATED and organised OPPOSITION,**
  religious in its intensity, *political* and *legal* in its broader aims and results ;—∴
    i. **Parliament** claimed to *share in Sovereignty*: to check the executive : to *impeach* ministers.
    ii. **Lawyers,** e.g. Coke, Hakewill, insisted that Prerogative was subject to the *Common Law*—a code superior to statutes, and independent of Kings.
    iii. **Puritans** fought for *liberty of choice*, especially in matters religious ; not from any King's dictation would they take their *creed, discipline,* or *style of worship.*

JAMES I 1603—1625.

HIS DESPOTISM — What INFLUENCES contributed to it?

I. **Tudors** supplied **precedents** for autocratic rule *
II. His **Title** seemed to him, and was by Parliament declared, to be **hereditary**: he was great-great-grandson of Henry VII; the will of Henry VIII, which preferred the Suffolks, was ignored.
III. His persuasion of a "**Divine Right.**"
IV. His **hatred of Presbyters,** who had been politically a nuisance to him in Scotland.
V. His **admiration for Spain,** the champion of his mother.
VI. His **immense conceit,** and lack of wise advisers after Cecil's death.

WHAT FORMS DID HIS DESPOTISM TAKE?

A. **PARLIAMENT** he provoked ∴
  I. Its **PRIVILEGES**—he insisted—**depended on his grace**:—
    ∴ as to
    (a) *Elections of M.P.'s*—he claimed to judge of a candidate's fitness; and that *Chancery* should revise returns; *Goodwin* had been elected for Bucks: James arranged an election of *Fortescue*, whom the Commons rejected.
    (b) *Liberty of Speech*:—for this he imprisoned 1614 Wentworth and 3 other M.P.'s. 1621 Coke, Selden, Pym, and Earl of Oxford.
    (c) *Liberty of Debate and Protest*:—as to the Spanish match 1621, he tore out protest from the journals.
  II. Its **FUNCTIONS**—he usurped, in the matter of **taxation** and **legislation,** as in the cases of
    (a) "**Impositions**" 1606:—i.e. **Bate,** a merchant, refused an *extra* Customs duty, which James imposed on currants; Exchequer Court decided for the King (∵ it was a *matter of State*: foreign trade belonged to "*prerogative*": ports are the King's gates—he may open them on his own conditions).
      ∴ James issued a "**Book of Rates**"; but the Commons, angrily protesting, made him withdraw it.
    (b) "**Proclamations,**" *altering the law*, e.g. 1610 he thus created the crime of making starch from wheat. Coke decided they were valid only if *admonitory* of existing law.

    III. Its **EXISTENCE** he **suspended** 1614—1620.

B. The COMMON LAW—he **hated** and **repudiated** ∵ lawyers pointed to it as a code independent of Kings, *limiting "prerogative"* ; ∴

    (a) The **Ordinary Courts**—he **degraded,** by exalting *Chancery,* the *Bishop's Courts, Star Chamber,* High Commission Court** ; he even claimed to decide legal disputes himself, as in the **Case of Prohibitions 1607 :** *King's Bench* had issued a "prohibition" to stop *Church Courts* hearing cases cognisable in lay courts ; James said *he* would settle the dispute ; but Coke said King had no such competence ;

    (b) The **Judges'** office he **debased ;** ∵ he charged them to urge payment of a *benevolence* ; and, by *writ " de rege inconsulto,"* he tried to stop their hearing of any matter touching his prerogative ; as in the **Case of Commendams 1616 :** Could a Bishop keep a living vacant ? Coke and other Judges, trying this question, ignored the King's writ : were summoned before him : Coke was stubborn, and, shortly after, ceased to be L.C.J.

    Now James had a *perfectly servile Bench.*

    (c) His **Subjects' liberties,** old as Magna Carta, he **violated** by

      (i) *Martial Law*—i.e. soldiers were commissioned to do summary justice even on common felons. A manifest thief he had, in 1603, executed without any trial.

      (ii) *Imprisonment*—for no valid cause, e.g. of 10 of the Millenary Petitioners, 1604 ; of Oliver St. John, who refused the benevolence, 1614.

      (iii) *Convictions* for treason on *flimsy evidence* ; e.g. *Raleigh* 1604, for supposed complicity in the "**Main plot**" and "**Bye plot**," to enthrone Arabella Stuart ; *Peacham* 1615, for an *unpublished* sermon, declaring James unfit to govern : no more than a seditious libel.

      (iv) *Exactions*—by Impositions, Loans, Benevolences.

C. NATIONAL SENTIMENT he **wounded** and **spurned :** by his

    (1) Sympathy with **Papists**—intolerance of Puritans.

    (2) Confiding in **favourites,** especially Robert Carr, and George Villiers.

    (3) **Apathy** over the **Elector Palatine's** cause, on which the Nation's heart was set.

    (4) **Courting Spain,** especially in the marriage project ; and Raleigh was executed 1618, to gratify Spanish vengeance.

CONSTITUTIONAL IMPORTANCE
OF JAMES I's REIGN.

A. UNION of ENGLISH and SCOTCH Crowns:
not *legislative* Union (until 1707) but *Executive*, ∴ e.g.
  (1) **No War** was possible between the two countries;
  (2) **Calvin's case** 1608:—were the "**Postnati**," e.g. Calvin, born in Scotland after the union, natural British subjects?—could they e.g. be *entitled to English land*? Coke held yes; ∵ **allegiance** was **personal**: both countries had the same *person* for King: ∴ both owed the same allegiance.

B. POLITICAL PARTIES became distinctly OPPOSED:

The COURT PARTY	v.	The COUNTRY PARTY
Led by *Bishops and Courtiers*:		Led by *Puritans and Lawyers*:
1. **Prerogative** to be absolute by Divine Right.		1. Prerogative to be **Limited** by the Common Law.
2. **Star Chamber** and H.C. Court the supreme organs of King's will.		2. **Parliament**, the highest Court, to share in Sovereignty.
3. Intolerance of **Puritans**.		3. Intolerance of **Papists** and of the **Episcopal system**.
4. **Judges** to be servile—"lions at the foot of the throne."		4. Judges **not to be coerced**.

C. DESPOTISM was ATTEMPTED *: BUT—so far was the nation from acquiescing, as under the Tudors:—

PREROGATIVE was **CURTAILED** or **CHALLENGED** by
  (a) The **Commons' resistance** to *Impositions* *: and to *Monopolies* *
  (b) **Coke's decisions** in the cases of *Prohibitions,* Proclamations,* Commendams.**

PARLIAMENT'S POWERS were CONFIRMED, in so far as
  I. **King's Title** was by it declared **Hereditary**, Henry VIII's will being overridden.
  II. **Privileges** were vindicated,* as *independent* of the King's grace.
  III. **Checks on the Executive** were exercised by the Commons by
    (i) **Impeachments** (revived 1621) for illegal conduct; esp. of *Bacon* 1621, *Middlesex* 1623.
    (ii) **Activity in Finance,** especially the
      (a) Resistance to Impositions, Monopolies, Feudal dues, and Purveyance.
      (b) Refusal of Supplies, e.g. 1614, until grievances were redressed.
      (c) Appointment of treasurers 1624 to account for the war fund voted.

But it was **not yet** (what Parliament later became) an active legislature—a King-making power—creator of ministries—identical practically with the Commons—controlling finance and army's existence—the organ of a self-governing democracy.

CHARLES I 1625—1649.

COURSE OF EVENTS
until the *Long Parliament* is summoned 1640.

A. THE KING calls 3 PARLIAMENTS 1625—1628 ;
but there is friction over

 (i) **Buckingham**—regarded as Charles' evil adviser ;
   ∴ Eliot started *impeachment* of Buckingham.

 (ii) **Tunnage and Poundage**—which the Commons voted to Charles for 1 year only.

 (iii) **" Privilege "** of the House—violated by Charles, e.g. his order to the Commons to " *adjourn.*"

 (iv) **Case of Darnel** 1627, one of the **" Five Knights,"** imprisoned by the Council for refusing the *Forced Loan* ; Court held " *King's special command* " a good return to the **Habeas Corpus Writ,** though no definite charge be specified, and though no trial be in view.

N.B. **1628 PARLIAMENT :—**

 First Session :—Grievances must precede grant of Subsidies ;
   ∴ Liberty of the subject in person and estate is discussed, and, led by *Wentworth, Pym,* and *Coke,* the Commons drafted, on *conservative* lines,

 The **" PETITION OF RIGHT "** : providing against

 I. Arbitrary Taxation : " Loan, Benevolence, Tax or such like charge "; " *De tallagio* " and statutes of Edward III and Richard III were cited. Did this cover *indirect* taxes ?

 II. Arbitrary Imprisonment : cf. *Darnel's* case.

 III. Billeting of Soldiers and Marines on private houses.

 IV. Martial Law Commissions—for trying soldiers *and others* by other than Common Law procedure.

 The Peers' suggestion of a clause saving " *King's Sovereign power* " was scouted by Coke, as implying a power superior to Law and Right. Charles assented to the Petition, at first evasively, finally in the usual form ;
 Thus it **became a " Statute."**

 Second Session :—" *Tunnage and Poundage* " was still exacted by Charles ;
 ∴ (a) **Rolle,** a merchant M.P. was distrained on for not paying. Judges held Charles justified by Bate's case, and not debarred by Petition of Right.
   ∴ Parliament wished to arraign at the bar the officers who had distrained, ∴ a *breach of Privilege.*
  ∴ Charles ordered the House to adjourn ;

∴ (b) **Three Resolutions**, moved by Eliot and Hollis were passed amid tumult, 1629 :—that those be deemed public enemies who were privy to
  (i) *Popish innovations* in religion ;
  (ii) *Tunnage and Poundage*—its collection or payment.

B. THE KING WITHOUT PARLIAMENT 1629—1640.

∴ **Personal** Despotism, his chief instruments being
Strafford (Wentworth), President of Council of the North :
Laud, Abp., active in High Commission Court : *
Noy, Attorney-General, who suggested Ship-money writs :
Finch, Lord Keeper, who extended Ship-money writs.

I. **Imprisonment** of Eliot, Hollis and others, for their attitude over the " three resolutions " 1629.

II. **Money** raised by various **illegal methods** ;
esp. by *Ship-money writs* 1634, 1635, 1636 ; extended even to inland counties :

∴ Case of **Hampden,** who refused to pay £1 ;
In Exchequer Chamber 7 judges to 5 held for the King : the rule of *government*, as distinct from *law*, arms him with a paramount power to meet necessity, of which he alone can judge.

III. **Proclamations** by the Council take the place of Statutes.

IV. **Star Chamber** * and **High Commission Court,** * overriding ordinary law, cruelly oppressed the King's opponents : e.g. **Prynne,** a Puritan lawyer, mutilated for his " *Histriomastix* " (an attack on stage-plays).

V. **Attack on the Scots' Religion** 1637. By forcing on them a Liturgy, he provoked their " *Covenant* " to resist episcopacy, and their " *Army of Invasion* " : to meet which, Charles needed money, ∴

C. **PARLIAMENT** again was summoned : hence the " **Short Parliament** " 1640 :—Moderate and restrained in temper, but, before " Supply," discussed King's attack on Religion, Privilege, Private property ; ∴ after 3 weeks, was dissolved by Charles, who resumed tyranny, called Strafford to his aid, was defeated by the Scots, and, when his army grew restive,
Summoned a **Council of Peers** at York ; but they could only advise him to call a new Parliament : hence

The " LONG PARLIAMENT " 1640 (Nov.)*

Of 504, the **majority** were determined **Puritans**. It lasted in theory till 1660, in fact till 1653 ; but, by then, it had become a mere remnant (" *Rump* "), and though at first " the sovereign of its sovereign, it ended as the servant of its servant," (the Army).

BY WHAT STAGES was the CRISIS approached?

(i) **Charles visits Scotland**—to win the Scots over, by pretence of sympathy with Presbyterianism, and to procure evidence for a treason charge against Pym. He tried to trap Argyll and Hamilton as Pym's confederates (the "*Incident*").

(ii) **Army Plot :**—His scheme to induce the Army chiefs to help him *coerce Parliament*, while he enlisted aid from Ireland, where Papists were massacring Protestants. Plot was revealed to Pym. ∴

(iii) **Grand Remonstrance** 1641 Nov.

An appeal by **Pym** to the nation :—

(a) *Vindicating*—against the Court, Peers and Papists—Parliament's authority and Protestant religion.

(b) *Answering* imputations on the Commons' atittude ; "We believe in conformity, but resist needless ceremonies, monuments of idolatry, and the temporal power of Bishops."

(c) *Demanding* securities against Popery—corrupt Judges—evil advisers ; King's ministers should be such as Parliament approves of.

Carried by a majority of 11 ; presented to Charles ; and, after some protest, printed.

(iv) **Attack on the Five Members** 1642 Jan. :—*Pym, Hampden, Hollis, Hazelrig, Strode*; after Charles tried and failed to lure Pym into accepting office,

(a) He tried *to Impeach Pym's party* for the "treason" of seducing Army, inviting a Scotch invasion, etc. ; but King is not competent to impeach ; Then

(b) He *invaded the House* with soldiers, meaning to arrest the five (who had fled), so that the Minority leaders with offices would have controlled the House.

(v) **Militia Bill,** 1642 Feb. :—To prevent Charles turning militia against Parliament, it was to be under *Parliament's* nominees. Charles refused assent : ∴ the House issued an "*Ordinance.*"

(vi) **The 19 Propositions** sent to Charles at York : e.g. Parliament to control all officials, the Militia, and marriages of the King's children. Charles refused ; ∴

PARLIAMENT at WAR with the KING :—

CIVIL WAR, i.e. **GREAT REBELLION, 1642—1648.***

THE LONG PARLIAMENT'S WORK?

by *Legislation—Grand Remonstrance—Ordinances* :—

HOW FAR did it anticipate MODERN principles?

I. Ministers to be Responsible to Parliament :—

∴ *Impeachment* and *Attainder* of Strafford and Laud, for their policy of "*Thorough*," in politics and religion.

II. Ordinary Common Law Courts to prevail :—

∴ (a) *Star Chamber, High Commission,* and some other special Courts—offshoots of Privy Council—were *abolished.*
(b) *Church Courts* must not fine, imprison, or inflict corporal punishment.
(c) *Judges* should administer the laws *unbiassed* by the King.

III. Parliament is a vital organ of government :—

∴ (i) *Triennial Act*—a Parliament must not, for over 3 years, be continued: or discontinued, else, Lord Chancellor, or Peers, or Sheriffs, or the People, shall arrange an election; and King must not end the *session* within 50 days.
(ii) The Long Parliament shall have a *veto on its own dissolution.*

IV. Subjects' **Personal Liberty** to be secured :—

∴ (a) *Impressment* for Army was declared illegal :
(b) On *Habeas Corpus writ,* even though a man is committed by Privy Council, Court shall scrutinise the cause.

V. Subjects' **Property** to be safe from arbitrary taxation :

∴ it declared illegal—the King's levy of Ship-money, Tunnage and Poundage, Distraint of Knighthood, and the Forest extensions.

VI. Church is subject to *Parliament's* intervention :—

∴ measures hostile to the Bishops.

Thus far, its work was **MAINLY CONSERVATIVE**, giving "*new force* to *old laws*" : restoring the pre-Tudor constitution.

BUT it broke with tradition, if not with **law,** in so far as

(a) It aimed at *divesting the Crown of Executive Power,* esp. of free choice of ministers, and control of militia.
(b) *Bishops* were *deprived of their votes* in House of Lords.
(c) *Attainder* of Strafford was to cover illegality of the treason charge.
(d) *Provisos* guarding the *Triennial Act* were revolutionary; so too the Parliament's veto on its own dissolution.
(e) "*Ordinances*" were issued by the Commons, e.g. for control of militia; forming the Court to try Charles; abolishing the House of Lords.

CAUSES OF THE GREAT REBELLION
1642—1648.

CHARACTER of Charles I. ?

I. His belief in Divine Right :
Instilled by his father, preached by Arminian clergy ; confirmed by servile judges, who ∴ attributed to him an authority paramount to Law.

II. His Casuistry ; ∴ the promises he gave as a *man* he felt he could repudiate as a *King* ; ∴ nobody could trust him. For kingship, at a critical period, such failings were fatal, his domestic virtues useless.

III. His obstinate confidence that he alone could be right :

∴ (a) He never tried to understand the Nation's hopes and sentiments ; nor could he, like Edw : I or Elizabeth, bend to popular opposition, or arrange a compromise between extremes.

(b) He shaped, and clung to, his own scheme of government, but, lacking the statecraft for carrying it through, he either took refuge in cunning and duplicity, or delegated to evil advisers the finding of means and methods, esp. to Wentworth and Laud, whose policy of "*Thorough*" meant the *forcing of arbitrary measures in the teeth of popular resistance*.

TYRANNY of Charles I ? It was *Political* and *Religious* : so ∴ were the **causes of the Civil War :—**

A. POLITICAL :—the principles at stake being those of

I. Parliament's Authority :—Was government to rest on the King's will as signified *by himself*, or the King's will as signified *through Parliament* ?
Charles refused to share sovereignty with Parliament :

∴ (i) Its *existence* he suspended 1629–1640 ; and legislated, instead, by "Proclamations."

(ii) Its *privileges* he violated, e.g. Order to adjourn, and attempt to arrest the 5 M.P.'s.

(iii) Its *control of taxation* he ignored in his illegal methods of raising money.

(iv) Its *endeavour to control the Executive* ; he hotly resented, when Parliament, remembering the examples of Buckingham, Wentworth, Laud, and the Cabinet meetings, and the **Army Plot**, demanded that

(a) *Ministers* should be approved by Parliament.
(b) *Militia* be put under Parliament's control.

II. Dignity of the Common Law and **Judges' independence;**
The *securities for Common Law justice* were *nullified*
by (a) Privy Council's arbitrary imprisonments.
   (b) Procedure of Star Chamber, Church Courts, and Martial Law.
   (c) Judges being privately sounded, or openly pressed, for decisions which placed Prerogative above the law: see cases of *Darnel, Rolle, Hampden.*

But on these merely *political* issues Charles could not have rallied a fighting party; too many of his well-wishers favoured *constitutional* reforms. So the force for driving the wedge deep, and **creating two hostile camps,** was found by Pym in more soul-stirring grievances, viz.:

B. RELIGIOUS:—His own creed and form of worship Charles was forcing upon all the Scots, and most of the English, who intensely detested, and joined in resisting them.

I. The **Scots**—as **Presbyterians**—*hated* the rule of *Bishops*, and any but their own austere style of worship;

but Charles, by giving their *Bishops political power* 1633, and forcing on them a *new Liturgy* 1637,

united against himself Scots Nobility, Kirk, and People.

II. The **English** majority—as **Puritans** *—were inclined to
   (a) Continental Protestantism of Calvin:
   (b) Suspicions of Episcopal rule and "popish innovations":
   (c) Liberty of Conscience:
   (d) Simplicity in religious services:

∴ Many favoured an *assimilation* of the English Church to the Scots' Presbyterian model.

But **Charles** and **Abp. Laud** insisted on
   (a) *Nationality and Unity* of the Anglican Church as vital to State solidarity: King having a right to control religion: Churchmen holding State offices.
   (b) *Episcopal discipline* and *jurisdiction*, centred in the hated **High Commission Court.***
   (c) *Denial* of the *right of private judgment*: conformity to the Laudian Articles and Liturgy, prescribing
   (d) *Ornate ritual*, vestments, altar at east end, etc.

∴ Firmly opposed any remodelling of the Church which would mean the downfall of Bishops—pillars of the Stuart throne.

EFFECTS OF THE GREAT REBELLION?

No permanent **organic change;** the failure of Cromwell's experiments proved the nation's bent to be towards **Monarchy.**

But certain **sentiments** were stirred, and **precedents** set, which marked the *lines on which the constitution would develop.*

A. SOVEREIGN POWER, clearly, could **not** be vested in an **Army,** a **Presbyterian oligarchy,** or an **irresponsible King**: *Divine Right* was discredited; the King must be *responsible*, as a *party* to a contract with his subjects; Hobbes' theory of Kingship must yield to Locke's.

B. PARLIAMENT established **records**—well sustained under Charles II, and partly foreshadowing its future greatness —for

    I. **Greater permanence** as an organ of government.
    II. **Intolerance** in religious matters.
    III. **Legislative activity,** independently of the King.
    IV. **Predominance of the Commons** over the Peers.
    V. **Control of the Executive**—it handled the revenue, took over the militia, and unmade a King.

C. PARTY SPIRIT intensified:—**Religious intolerance** was long to inflame the strife of political parties;

    (1) *Romanism* was finally rejected as a national creed; Protestantism was more firmly rooted; *yet*
    (2) *Puritans*, by reaction after their triumph, entered on a period of depression; while the status of Protestant Dissenters was growing more distinct.
    ∴ (3) *Anglican Church* begins to be *no longer* the Church of the *nation*, but only of the *majority*.

D. MILITARISM becomes emphatically **ODIOUS**; hence lively **suspicions,** after 1660, of a **Standing Army**—so handy a lever of royal tyranny, as it had been of a dictator's.

E. PETITIONING King or Parliament, with a view to influencing legislation, became a common practice from this period.

F. DREAD of a recurrence **OF CIVIL WAR**

    (a) Drew the *moderates* into a temporary *coalition* for restoring the Monarchy; and
    (b) Kept Charles II to a policy of *prudent caution*.

THE PRIVY COUNCIL
in the "Age of Councils" 1461—1641.

After 1461, with the "**New Monarchy**" of Edward IV, and the **Tudor period**, we reach the "golden age" of the Privy Council.

A. Composed mainly of **COMMONERS**—it was

∴ **dependent on the King** who exalted them; while the post of "*Secretary*" or "*President*" offered unique distinction to royal deputies like T. Cromwell, Somerset, Burleigh, Strafford.

B. SERVILE INSTRUMENT of Tudor Sovereigns,

whose despotism it veiled, and whose vast powers,* it exercised, as the **Chief Organ of Government**, either in full Council, or through some branch or committee, viz.:

  I. **Council of Wales**—created under Edw: IV; confirmed 1542; sat at Ludlow, with jurisdiction paramount as to Wales and the "Marches," e.g. Salop.

  II. **STAR CHAMBER.***

  III. **Court of Delegates** 1534, for *Ecclesiastical* and *Admiralty* appeals; lasted until 1832.

  IV. **Council of the North** 1537—sat at York, as a Star Chamber for the north.

  V. **Regency Council,** under Somerset, temp. Edw: VI.

  VI. **COURT OF HIGH COMMISSION.***

C. SUPERSEDED PARLIAMENT'S authority

over more than half the realm; for it could alter the law by "**Ordinances**"; and "**Proclamations**," to which the validity of Statute was given by Parliament under Hen: VIII.

D. ENCROACHED ON the province of COMMON LAW COURTS:

so that Right and Justice came to depend

Not on **Judges** sworn to disregard royal mandates, enforcing a Common Law independent of King's will;

But on **Politicians** sworn to observe the King's counsel; inspired by royal caprice, or the policy of the day: *discretionary*, unfettered by any fixed procedure.

BUT under the **first two Stuarts,** in proportion as

Parliament resumed its old vitality, and

Common Law was vindicated by Lawyers, and

Prerogative rule was challenged,

Government by "Councils" was doomed to end; so, after the tyrannous excesses of Star Chamber and High Commission Court under Charles I,

  Long Parliament 1640 abolished **B. I, II, IV, VI**;

thus **PRIVY COUNCIL** was reduced to little more than a body of **POLITICAL ADVISERS to the Crown**; and even in this character it was soon to be superseded by **a new committee** of itself, i.e. the **CABINET.***

THE COMMONWEALTH 1649—1660.

Constitutional experiments : **Why did they fail ?**

A. The **ARMY,** the "**RUMP,**" and a "**COUNCIL OF STATE,**"
   i.e. 41 officers and M.P.'s, including Cromwell,
   I. **Co-operated** at first, while danger threatened from Ireland and Loyalist risings here ;
   II. **Quarrelled** later—**Army** and **Rump** wishing each to be rid of the other ; and an *Army* section—" *Levellers* "—wanted *democracy* ;
   "**Rump**" posed as a Sovereign, and favoured **oligarchy.**
   ∴ Cromwell forcibly dissolved it, 1653.

B. **BAREBONE'S** Puritan **CONVENTION** of 144 " Saints," **nominated** by Cromwell ; but
   too bent on " **overturning** " *Church, Lawyers, Landowners,* ∴ offended Cromwell's conservatism—would multiply his foes ; ∴ resigned its powers to him.

C. **THE PROTECTORATE** was next **founded** 1653 by "**Instrument of Government**"—a "*paper*" constitution, drafted by Lambert and other officers :
   (1) Cromwell to be " **Protector** " : advised by a
   (2) **Council of 21,** to be his nominees later on ;
   (3) **National Parliament,** of **one Chamber,** for E.S.I., elected triennially by all, exc. papists.

∴ **1654** a "*Parliament,*" elected on the new system ; but republican M.P.s wished to reduce the powers of Cromwell, who ∴ dissolved it.

1656 a new "*Parliament*"—purged by Cromwell of 100 republicans. The remnant then framed

D. " **HUMBLE PETITION and ADVICE** " :—
   (i) **Parliament** to be again of **Two Houses :**
   (ii) Cromwell to be " **King** " (∵ *a title limited by well-known precedents*)—**nominate** the **Upper** House, and appoint his **successor.**

∴ **1658** a "*Parliament*" of 2 Houses ; but the 100 attended ; the Lower House repudiated the Upper ; ∴ dissolved by Cromwell ; then he died.

E. **Richard Cromwell,** made Protector **by the Council 1659,** had a "*Parliament*" elected on the old style ; but the **Army** was now **predominant :**

∴ (a) *Colonel Lambert* made him dissolve it, and recalled the Rump. Lambert's clique quarrelled.
   (b) *General Monk* recalled the original " Long Parliament," which issued writs for the
   (c) " **Convention** " Parliament 1660, strong in " moderates " ; which—*Monk* negotiating with Prince Charles " *Declaration of Breda* "—**restored the Monarchy.**

WHY DID CROMWELL FAIL?

A. **He failed to realise** that the **REBELLION was AGAINST NOT KINGSHIP,** but a **particular King**: that the nation's bent was towards *precedent*, and *legalism*; even a popular hero could hardly have stirred loyalty to a military *Dictator* and a "*paper*" Constitution. But in fact

B. **HIS UNPOPULARITY** steadily **increased** :—

∴ (1) **Military rule** offended all Civilians; **Martial Law** had been one of the Stuart iniquities.

(2) To *Cavaliers* he seemed the **arch-regicide**: for the *Presbyterians* he was **too tolerant**; for the *Army* **too conservative**; *yet* he was **too dependent on Army** to be acceptable, as a leader, to the *moderates.*

(3) **His dogmatic religion** repelled all but a few.

Thus he was ill qualified to unite into one body of supporters

C. **FACTIONS, so numerous,** divided on *religion* and *politics*, with mutually destructive programmes :—

  I. **PAPISTS** (*royalists*).

  II. **EPISCOPALIANS** (*royalists*), who stood for Church government by bishops.

  III. **PURITANS,** who were split into

   (a) "**Presbyterians**" (many *royalist*), who would replace bishops with a tyranny of Presbyters, intolerant of dissent.

   (b) "**Independents,**" mostly *republicans*, who favoured State recognition of *all* Protestant sects :—

    (i) **Cromwell** and his ring :
    (ii) Mass of **the Army,** who resented the rule of any "*single*" person :
    (iii) "**Saints,**" who posed as an oligarchy divinely inspired for reforms :
    (iv) "**Levellers,**" i.e. social democrats, who would level all ranks and orders.

∴ D. **PARLIAMENT NOT WORKABLE**: it could **NOT** be
  United—when the nation was so divided;
  Trustful of a dictator ever ready to end it by force;
  Allowed a freedom it might use to restore the Stuarts
  Expected to support a "*paper*" constitution, which it had no hand in shaping.

CHARLES II 1660—1685.

MOTIVES AND FEATURES OF HIS POLICY?

I. SECURITY of his throne :
  to avoid "going on his travels" again :—
  ∴ (a) **His fear of re-awakening the spirit of rebellion ;**
    ∴ he never pushed a crisis too far, e.g. as to the "*Indulgence.*"
  (b) **His leaning to Popery, as Politic ;** a self-assertive Puritanism upset his father's throne : his own might be safer, if supported by a religion of self-suppression.

II. Pursuit of his own VICES and LUXURIES :
  Money voted for the navy was diverted to private uses.

III. HEREDITARY RIGHT of the Stuarts to be maintained ;
  ∴ he resisted the "*Exclusion Bill,*" which would shut out his Papist brother and Protestant nieces.

IV. Ambition of being INDEPENDENT OF PARLIAMENT :
  ∴ he lazily reached towards Absolutism,

  (a) **By TACTICS secret and subtle—**
    (i) *Selling himself* to Louis XIV for an income ;
    (ii) *Assenting to persecuting statutes,* to make Parliament odious to dissenters ;
    (iii) *Playing off* one party against another, so as always to have *one* on his own side ;
    (iv) *Dissolving* Parliament, so as to stop it from carrying a measure through ;
    (v) *Bribing* the Parliamentary Opposition into silence.

  (b) **By UNCONSTITUTIONAL MOVES,** *savouring of despotism* :—
    (i) **Standing Army** was kept, and increased.
    (ii) **Cabinets** were persisted in ; how could he work his intrigues with a Privy Council of 50, or even 30 ?
    (iii) **Imprisonments** of troublesome subjects, e.g. *Jenkes*, a "petitioner," in evasion of the Habeas Corpus Writ.
    (iv) **Suspending** Statutes, claimed as a prerogative by "Declaration of Indulgence."
    (v) **Pardoning,** with intent to bar impeachment ; would *defeat the responsibility of Ministers.*
    (vi) **Attack on the Towns' Charters** with "*Quo Warranto Writ*" ; he packed the judges to make sure of the decision, and new Charters were so framed, that the Crown could *influence the returns* of M.P.'s.
    (vii) **Design to upset** the Protestant **Church.**

HOW FAR, by 1660, WAS THE MODERN CONSTITUTION APPARENT?

A. KINGSHIP was more **RESPONSIBLE**, not **Absolute**; in contrast with the Monarchy of James I or Henry VIII, "**Prerogative**" was no longer *discretionary*, but **limited by Law. YET**

   I. Charles II could still attempt **PERSONAL RULE:**
   by Dispensing and Suspending powers:
   Destroying old Town Charters:
   Dissolving Parliament capriciously:
   Bribing M.P.'s to overcome the Opposition:
   Allying with one faction, to overcome another.

   And he had **some advantages over his predecessors,**
   viz. *Standing Army*, small, but growing:
      Cabinet Meetings, facilitating a secretive policy:
      Press Control, under the Licensing Law:
      Memory of Civil War, making agitators cautious.

But **II. ROYAL POWER had been REDUCED** in so far as

   (a) **Privy Council** supremacy, and arbitrary **Courts**, had ceased:
   (b) **Arbitrary Taxation** disappears; Parliament fixes the Crown's **Civil List**.
   (c) **Proclamations** legislative become **rare**.
   (d) **Bishops cease** to be tools of despotism.
   (e) **New Boroughs** were not created after 1666.

B. PARLIAMENT had acquired **some** of its modern characteristics and activities;

   It **SUSTAINED the** spirit of the **LONG PARLIAMENT NOT** when at first, in a fervour of *loyalty*,
      it *restored* the Bishops and House of Lords:
      gave back to the Crown Militia and Press control:
      declared legislation needed King's assent;

   BUT in the matter of
   I. Legislative energy;
      not absorbed in protests and quarrels with King.

   II. Party Spirit intense;
      ∴ vindictive **persecution** now *of*, not *by*, Puritans; and over the *Exclusion Bill* began the modern division of **political parties**.

   III. Security for personal liberty—re-affirmed in the **Habeas Corpus** Act 1679.

   IV. Abolition of feudal dues, and the substitution of a "*Civil List*."

   V. Hostility to a Standing Army at the King's call.

VI. Challenging the foundation of Royalty ;
∴ the *Exclusion Bill* raised the old question—not settled until 1688—*was the Crown merely the "appurtenance of a pedigree,"* or an office tenable only by the **nation's** selected **agent?**

VII. The Commons' resistance to the Lords *
  (a) Amending a Money Bill.
  (b) Original jurisdiction in torts: *Skinner v. E. India Co.* 1667.
  (c) Hearing appeals from Chancery: *Shirley v. Fagg* 1675.

VIII. Enlarging its control over the **Executive** :—
  (a) **Ministers' responsibility** to Parliament was re-affirmed in *impeachments* of Clarendon and Danby.
  (b) **Reform of Privy Council** was attempted on *Temple's* plan, giving Parliament a large share in selecting King's advisers.
  (c) **Wider control of Finance,** ∴
    (1) *Civil List* was instituted, i.e. in place of Feudal dues, an annual allowance from Parliament to King (to Charles £1,200,000, out of Customs and Excise).
    (2) *Money-Bills* were declared *not* to be *amendable* by the Lords.
    (3) *Clergy lost* the privilege of self-taxation.
    (4) *Appropriation of supplies* by the Commons in 1665.
    (5) *Account* and *Audit* of expenditure was insisted on.

Thus our **modern Revenue system** * was foreshadowed.

FOREIGN RELATIONS under CHARLES II.

Foreign influences on English politics were powerful, and shifted according as *National sentiment*, or the *King's intrigues*, prevailed ;

A. As to the DUTCH—English *sentiment* was *mixed* :
  I. Jealousy of them as our **trade rivals**
    in *shipping*, in the *Indies*, in American *colonisation* ;
  ∴ (a) **War v. Holland** 1665–1667, Clarendon being minister ; our navy, under Monk and Prince Rupert, was defeated by de Ruyter. Dutch sailed up our rivers. By *Peace of Breda* the Navigation Act was modified ; we acquired "New Amsterdam," i.e. New York State.
  (b) **Impeachment of Clarendon** followed, for misconduct of the war, etc. He was banished.

II. Sympathy with them as **Calvinistic Protestants,** esp. felt by *Shaftesbury* and the *Dissenters*;

∴ (a) **Triple Alliance** 1668 arranged by Shaftesbury: i.e. league of England, Holland, Sweden, to check Louis XIV;

Charles ∴ countered this with the secret "**Treaty of Dover**" 1670.

(b) **Unpopularity of 2nd War** v. Holland 1672–1674 (waged by Charles in support of Louis), when we realised we were aiding a *Popish despotism* against a *Protestant republic*.

B. As to the FRENCH :—

I. Charles uniformly **courted Louis XIV ;**

encouraged in this by **Clarendon,** and by some of the Cabal; he hoped to be *independent of Parliament* by French gold, and French arms, and to *re-establish Popery* here; hence

(a) He married Catharine of Portugal :
(Portugal was a protégé of Louis.)

(b) Secret "Treaty of Dover," in pursuance of which,

(c) His "Declaration of Indulgence" followed.

(d) Dutch War 1672–1674 to promote Louis' plan of absorbing the Netherlands, so that he could menace Holland itself.

But **II.** Our **National antipathy to Charles' French policy** was reflected in

(i) Clarendon's impeachment:

(ii) Shaftesbury's anti-popery moves, viz. *Triple Alliance—Test Acts—"Popish Plot"* rumour—*Exclusion Bill*.

(iii) Danby's patriotic policy—*to wean Charles from France*—successful for an interval, so that war v. France seemed likely, and Mary married the deadly enemy of Louis;

but **Louis,** whose game lay in *fomenting political discord here*, retaliated by divulging Danby's letter, which indirectly caused the fall of the Cavalier Parliament.

N.B. William of Orange helped to defeat the *Exclusion Bill*.

JAMES II 1685—1688
a declared Papist.

WHAT CIRCUMSTANCES FAVOURED HIS ABSOLUTISM?

I. **Whigs** were now **humbled** and harmless; the "*Exclusion Bill*" had failed; the *hereditary principle* seemed *secure*.

II. **Weary of wrangling,** the majority of the **nation** was devoted to royalty, and disposed to Non-resistance; **Charles** had died a **popular King.**

III. **Parliament** was **tractable** in matters **non-religious;**
∴ (a) *Dissolutions*, frequent under Charles, had chastened it;
(b) *Town Charters' revision* enabled Crown to secure a strong *Tory* element in the *Commons*;
∴ it voted James a life annuity of nearly £2,000,000, which, with gold from Louis, made him independent.

IV. **Rebellions** of Monmouth and Argyle, which were easily suppressed, **stimulated loyalty,** and gave him an *excuse for enlarging the Army*.

V. **James** was **supported**
at home by a standing army of 3,000:
by the scandalous remnant of Charles' court:
by a Jesuit clique, and fanatical Irish Papists;
abroad by Louis XIV, his patron, model, and paymaster.

VI. The **Anglican** *versus* **Dissenter** feud seemed to offer a chance for the **Papist** to figure as "*tertius gaudens.*"

VII. **Dispensing power** (his favourite weapon) was *then*, in some degree, lawful, if confined to *individual* cases of peculiar hardship under certain Statutes.

VIII. **Mary,** his daughter (and **heiress** till 1688), being a **Protestant,** those who otherwise might have agitated at once, were *content to lie quiet till the Papist was dead*.

EVENTS LEADING UP
to the "GREAT REVOLUTION" 1688.

Arbitrary rule of James II?

I. **CUSTOMS** and **EXCISE** he raised *before Parliament had renewed its sanction*, which expired at Charles' death.

II. "**BLOODY ASSIZE,**" under **Jeffreys, C.J.**, assisted by Col. Kirke, i.e. after Monmouth's rebellion in the west, 350 rustics and miners were hanged, and nearly 1,000 were sent into slavery.

- **III. STANDING ARMY** was **increased** to 3,000, to overawe London and Parliament; trials by "**Martial Law**" were common.

- **IV. POPISH POLICY : attack on the Anglican Church :—**
  For his Council he had a cabal of Papists and Jesuits, e.g. Tyrconnel and father Petre; and *in defiance of Test Act* he **gave Papists offices,** military and civil.

  - **N.B.** the **legal status** of **Papists** and **Dissenters** then involved the
    - (a) *Positive* cruelty of **Penal laws** (e.g. *Conventicle Act*), prompted by bigotry, which *prohibited and punished* any worship other than Anglican;
    - (b) *Negative* evil of **Tests,** which barred from **Offices** and from **Parliament**
      - (i) *Papists,* ∴ deemed by patriots to be a peril to the State and Church.
      - (ii) *Protestant Dissenters*, whose ostracism was desired by their adversaries in party *politics*.

- **A. TEST ACT of 1673 he attacked first :—**
  Repeal of it—Parliament would not permit, ∴ was prorogued, never to re-assemble in his reign.
  ∴ *Evasion* of it—he effected, by procuring a packed court of Judges to decide the "**Dispensing power**" was lawful even for this :—
  ∴ **Godden v. Hales** 1686 : a collusive suit by an informer (servant of H.) ∴ H., a Papist, took a military office without complying with Test Act; his plea of King's "*Dispensation*" was held *good*.

- **B. "COURT OF ECCLESIASTICAL COMMISSION" 1686,**
  i.e. to promote Popery, a Board of 7, under Jeffreys, Ld. Chr., illegally revived the *High Commission Court*, whose seal and jurisdiction it adopted; thus
  Some Bishops, e.g. Compton, were deprived of their sees :
  Universities were attacked, e.g. Papist Heads were forced upon 2 Oxford Colleges.

- **C. PENAL LAWS** and the "**TESTS**" were **overthrown** by usurped prerogative of a "**SUSPENDING POWER,**" which, if allowed, could not be confined to laws of religion, and ∴ would *neutralise Parliament's legislative function*.

  - **I. His design,** as Papists were few, was **to win over Dissenters** by an insidious offer of *toleration* : thus to embroil them with Anglicans, and, after fusion of these, the *Papists* would, he hoped, *absorb both*.
  - ∴ **II.** By "**Declaration of Indulgence**" **1687** he made a clean sweep of the **Penal Laws** and **Tests,** with an order that it be read in all churches;
    - but (a) *Dissenters* rejected the bait, offered by a method which menaced civil liberty.
    - (b) 7 *Bishops* petitioned him not to require them to have it read in churches;

∴ **III. Trial of the 7 Bishops 1688;** prosecuted for their petition as a *seditious libel,* defended by Somers, they were acquitted amid general rejoicing, even of the Army.

The **trial**—decided, by implication, that
there *is* a *Right of Petitioning* Crown :
there *is no* prerogative of *Suspending Laws.*

The **occasion**—drew together Tories and Whigs, champions of the Church and lovers of Liberty, to vindicate the **Protestant Religion** and the **Law of the Constitution.**

Thus was consolidated a **NATIONAL RESISTANCE** to the **CROWN,** and this was spurred on by the **Birth,** to James and his 2nd wife, **of a Prince,** who would displace Mary as heir to the throne, and *certainly be a Papist.*

The events immediately following constituted

THE REVOLUTION of 1688.

COURSE OF THE REVOLUTION OF 1688?

I. INVITATION to **William of Orange,** by *Tories* and *Whigs* ;

What considerations had William to weigh?

(a) It was a *treasonable conspiracy* against his father-in-law ;

(b) Would *Tory Churchmen* really dethrone the Lord's Anointed ?

(c) If he imported *Dutch soldiers* to drive out an English King, would not all *Patriots be roused* to protest ?

(d) Called in as a mere "*political necessity,*" could he expect *loyalty* ? And if Mary was a focus for loyalty, would be himself be more than chief gentleman-in-waiting ?

(e) Dare he leave *Holland exposed* to attack from Louis ?

But he needed the aid of England's might against Louis ; and Louis just then was diverting his troops to the upper Rhine.

∴ **II. WILLIAM ARRIVES.** James, deserted by Anne, Sunderland, Churchill, and most of the Army, **fled** to France ; ∴ it was possible to pretend he had *abdicated.*

III. AN ASSEMBLY meets—of Peers, London Aldermen, and those in London who had sat in Charles' Parliament ; this advises William (though not yet King) to summon a

IV. "CONVENTION," 1688, of Peers, and elected M.P.'s.

Various parties and **plans** were represented :—

- **A. Ultra-Jacobites**—would restore James as an autocrat.
- **B. Ultra-Democrats**—would revert to a Commonwealth.
- **C. Tories** who wanted James back as a "*limited*" King.
- **D. Tories** who urged a *Regency*, deeming James insane.
- **E. Tories,** e.g. Danby, who, as James had abdicated, and his son seemed illegitimate, wished *Mary to be Queen*, ∵ *hereditary right* so demanded.
- **F. WHIGS**—who argued
    - (i) **Throne was vacant,** ∵ James had **forfeited** it by subverting the laws, and breaking his contract with his subjects ;
    - ∴ (ii) **Election** of a new King was necessary—by the *Nation*, ∴ **by Parliament ;**
    this view prevailed in the Commons : Peers finally agreed.

This "**Convention**" drafted the **DECLARATION OF RIGHTS * ;** and, after William and Mary had accepted the Crown on these terms, it voted itself to be transformed into a "**Parliament,**" though *no Royal writs* had summoned it ;

this passed the **BILL OF RIGHTS.***

THE "DECLARATION OF RIGHTS" 1689,

Intended to embody the **terms of the contract,** by which the Nation *engaged a new Royal family* : it "made nothing law that was not law before."

- **I. Recited the misdeeds** of James II, and how, by his abdication, the *throne was vacant*.
- **II. Declared** our ancient indubitable **liberties** to be :—
    - **A. King** must not, without Parliament's sanction, *Suspend laws* : *Dispense* "as of late" : *Levy taxes* : Keep a *Standing Army* : Erect a *High Commission Court*.
    - **B. Parliament** shall be held frequently ; and *freedom of speech* therein shall be undisputed.
    - **C. Subjects** have a Right
        to *Petition* King : to Freedom in *Elections* : to *Keep Arms*, if Protestants : to *Bail* not being excessive : to *Juries* being *properly qualified*.
- **III. Declared** William and Mary accepted the Crown on these terms.

IV. Settled the Crown on them, then on issue of Mary, then on Anne and her issue, then on William's issue by a later wife.

V. Imposed new Oaths of Allegiance and Supremacy, to replace such as had been sworn to the Stuarts.

THE "BILL OF RIGHTS" 1689,

Re-embodied all the above, and **added**

(a) **No Papist,** nor anyone married to Papist, shall **occupy Throne.**

(b) **New Sovereign,** at or soon after Coronation, **shall declare** against *Transubstantiation*, the *Mass*, and the *Adoration of the Virgin*.

(c) **Dispensing Power** is *absolutely* illegal,
   except if the Statute in question permits it: and
   except in cases to be specified in an Act to be passed that session: (no such Act was passed).

JUSTIFICATION for the REVOLUTION of 1688?

A. STRICTLY, it was AGAINST THE LAW of the Constitution; for though

(1) the *Fiction* was that the **Throne was Vacant** ∵ James had either by breach of contract **forfeited** it, *or* by flight **abdicated** for himself and his heirs, (this theory soothed the misgivings of believers in Divine Right),

(2) the *Fact* was he was **forced to go;** the invitation to William was **treasonable;** there was even **no Parliament** existing at the time;
no legal competence attached to the "**Convention**," nor to the "**Parliament**" which it resolved itself to be; how then could this *legally* create a King?

B. It was JUSTIFIABLE, however, in the light of

I. Historical precedents :
∵ the *elective* basis of English Kingship * was never wholly obscured; and note the depositions of Edward II and Richard II.

II. Political philosophy—for the ultimate source of all Sovereign authority must be the *assent of the People*.

III. Morality—for bad Kings have no *moral* right to govern; and when the better part of the community approves of *changing its governing Chief*, it is *ipso facto* morally right to rebel *pro tanto*. And

C. From non-legal conditions a **LEGAL** institution **may emerge;** the Nation's elected Head becomes a **King de jure,** as soon as the **Judges** are ready, and the **Executive** is able, to *give effect to laws issued in his name*; and the newly created **Sovereign can,** to satisfy *legalists*, **validate retrospectively** the process of the revolution, as was done by the Parliament proper of 1690.

HOW DID THE REVOLUTION of 1688 DIFFER from the GREAT REBELLION of 1642—1648 ?

I. A **National movement :**
   No split of the nation into two hostile camps.

II. Though **religion** in both crises supplied the chief momentum, it was now **a mightier impulse ;** ∴ instead of a feud within the Church, we find a *Patriotic Protestantism* defiant of *Popery from France.*

III. **Bloodless** almost ; and civil law and justice were undisturbed.

IV. **No change,** even temporary, in the **Form of Government ;** the Nation merely changed the tenant of its Throne, restoring old conditions of the tenancy, and refusing to be tied to a particular royal pedigree.

THE REVOLUTION of 1688.

ITS CONSTITUTIONAL IMPORTANCE ?

How has the Constitution changed since ?

It registered the results of Parliament's long struggle with the Stuart Kings : of the battle between

Liberty and **Autocracy :**
National Interests and **Royal Intrigues :**
Law and a **Vague Prerogative ;**

so that the Constitution resumed the character it bore prior to Edward IV ; but not as yet could it be described as merely a " *Crowned Republic.*"

A. **PARLIAMENT** was to be **no longer a mere critic** of, or **check** upon, the Crown ; it became, *jointly with the King,* **THE SOVEREIGN BODY,** and the *balance of power* lay with it ;

∴ **Undisputed,** by 1688, was **its right**
   to **depose** or **enthrone** Kings :
   to **liberty of debate :**
   to unlimited **legislative scope :**
   to **control the Executive,**
      by *impeachment*, which King may not bar :
      by *control of finance* : n.b. " Appropriation " :
      by determining the *Army's existence.*

BUT it was **not until after 1688** that

I. It became truly *Representative* and *Democratic* ;

II. It submitted to *Press criticism*, and *publication of debates* ;

III. Its *leaders* were, as of course, the chief *Executive* ;

IV. Its function of *Legislation* surpassed *Administration,* as the chief work expected of Government :

V. The " *Commons* " *predominated* over the " *Lords.*"

B. **THE MONARCHY** was to be no longer a matter of "*Divine Right*," nor a mere "*Birthright*," but

   (a) **Parliamentary :** ∴ the vacancy of the throne necessitated Parliament investing a new line with royalty; and

   (b) **Implying a Contract,** of which the *terms* can be found in the Declaration of Rights, and the *philosophy* in the writings of Locke.

   Thus for England was secured a **CONSTITUTIONAL KING** —a "**REX Politicus.**"

   BUT it was **not until after 1688** that the King's **personal influence** on government so far **declined** that he

   I. Lost the power to *dismiss Judges*, and to *choose his Ministers* :

   II. Had to *waive his Veto* on legislation :

   III. Ceased to *attend the Cabinet* :

   IV. Must do *official* acts only through the agency, and on the initiative, of *Ministers*.

C. **MINISTERS' RESPONSIBILITY,** as **servants** rather **of the Nation,** than of the **King,** was a recognised principle;

   Cabinets were a novelty of the period;

   BUT it was **not until after 1688** that

   I. Our *modern Cabinet system* developed * : and

   II. *Ministers* became *dependent* on, and responsible to, the Majority in the *House of Commons* :

   III. *Party Government* * became the rule.

D. **THE PEOPLE** benefited by the triumph of certain **Whig** and **Puritan principles.**

   Toleration, for Protestants, as to religious worship; Right of **Petitioning** was affirmed; and a less restricted **Press** was in view;

   BUT not until after 1688 did we reach *Civil* Toleration : full liberty to *Criticise Government* : real *Freedom in Elections* : free *Public Meetings* : and some sense of *Self-Government*.

PURITANISM

as a force in Politics.

As the *Reformation* was a revolt against *Papal authority*, so the **Puritans** asserted, in an *individualistic* spirit, a right of private judgment, resenting **Royal dictation** in matters religious.

A. As a RELIGIOUS MOVEMENT—it began with those who fled to the continent from Marian persecutions, and there learnt, from Calvinists and Huguenots,

> *Simplicity in worship*—∴ no ornate ritual :
> *Democratic Church rule*—∴ no Bishops :
> *Austere standards of conduct*—∴ e.g. no theatres.

Returning under Elizabeth, they took a stand as

I. Objectors to Prayer-Book uniformity—e.g. use of surplice, ring, cross, images ;

(a) *Strong in the Middle Classes*, who were no longer led by Church or Baronage ; ∴ the Puritans took an *independent* position ; *strong in the House of Commons*, where e.g. Cope and Strickland fought for reform of the Church *by Parliament*, thus ending Parliament's long acquiescence in Tudor autocracy.

∴ (b) *Odious to the Queen,* and to most of the *Bishops,* as offending her ecclesiastical supremacy :

> her taste for discipline and order :
> the organic unity of the Church.

∴ (c) *Persecuted* by the **High Commission Court** * ; and so they became the declared

II. Foes of Episcopacy ; n.b. the " *Marprelate* " Tracts. But *Crown and Bishops* were allied more than ever under **James I,** who deemed Bishops, the preachers of non-resistance, to be the pillars of his throne ;

∴ he **fiercely oppressed the Puritans,** who thus were constrained to fight

B. As a POLITICAL OPPOSITION to Stuart Despotism :—
Champions of constitutional Liberty, their fiery zeal inflamed the **creed of the 17th-century Popular Party,** viz.—

> *Parliament to be supreme : Episcopacy to be overhauled :*
> *Prerogative to be restricted : Popery to be suppressed :*
> *Divine Right to be scouted : Conscience to be free.*

I. Triumphant in the Civil War, over tyranny political and religious ; note the work of the *Long Parliament,* led by the Puritan Pym. But, after this extravagant success, they became

II. **Weakened** by the split into "*Presbyterians*" and "*Independents*"; hence a loss of cohesion, which led to their *decline* as a *political* party;

∴ III. **Persecuted**, for their *schism*, during the High Church reaction under Charles II; see the "**Clarendon Code,**" which drove out of the Church numbers who now, as "**Dissenters**," marched with the new **Whig Party**;

IV. **Vindicated** again **in the 1688 Revolution,** in so far as that established principles then accepted by an almost united nation, viz. :—

> a *Protestant England*:
> a *Sovereign Parliament*:
> a *Restricted Prerogative*: and
> some *freedom in* Protestant *worship*.

BUT not until the 19th century were the Puritan ideals further realised in *Civil Toleration*, more *Purity in politics*, a really *Free Press*, Free *Criticism of Government*, and a *predominant House of Commons*.

FEUDAL LAND LAW.

What features of our Constitution are **traceable to it?**

A. **TERRITORIAL character of British SOVEREIGNTY,** which replaced the older idea of Sovereignty as "**personal**"

(i.e. a power over *only the members* of a certain nation, *but* over these *even if abroad*);

∴ it followed from the feudal idea of the King as Lord paramount of all *English land*, *not* merely King of the *English*; and from it was derived

I. **Jurisdiction over all,** *even aliens*, within the realm, and not, generally, over anyone, even a subject, *if abroad*. And the exercise of this, esp. the sending of Judges on circuit, led to the early formation of *strong Central Government*.

II. **Proprietary** idea of **Kingship** *—
the basis of several of the Royal "*Prerogatives*," and prevalent as late as the Tudor period.

III. **Nationality** as dependent, by Common Law, upon **birth** on the **soil,** *not* upon *parentage*.

B. **HEREDITARY character of our MONARCHY,** and **LAY PEERAGE** *;

resulted from the feudal policy of keeping land tenure *undivided*; ∴ not to be devised by will; hence a *necessary intestacy*, and *singular* heirship by *primogeniture*; cf. note on "**Baronage by tenure.**"*

C. From such *INCIDENTS of FEUDAL TENURE* as **FEALTY ; HOMAGE ; SERVICES** due to, **PROTECTION** expected from, the *LORD*—have been derived

    I. Our theory of **Allegiance,** and ∴ of **Treason**—a breach of the fealty due to the Lord paramount from a subject or resident alien.

    II. The **incompetence of the Crown,** i.e. the "*Executive*" apart from Statute, **to expel** from the realm any subject or alien ; for this would mean a *denial of protection.*

    III. The **composition** of our **House of Lords,**
        in so far as the *ancient* qualification for a special writ was *Tenure*-in-chief, lay or ecclesiastical ;
        Many present peers are the heirs of those so qualified ; and Bishops are still members.

    IV. Hereditary Crown **Revenue** (feudal dues) and a **military force** (feudal array)—which, until 1661, secured to the Crown some independence of Parliament.
        The **royal "Demesnes"** remain, though no longer under the King's control.

N.B. Some Statutes, primarily effecting a change in *Land-law,* remotely had "*Constitutional*" results :—

DE DONIS 1285
made land inalienable, if granted "*to A and the heirs of his body.*" Hence vast domains converged in the hands of Barons, whose power *threatened the monarchy* until 1461.

QUIA EMPTORES 1290
stopped *subinfeudation* ; ∴ multiplied the Crown's *direct* tenants, thus *cheapening* the status of a *Tenant-in-chief.*

STATUTE OF TENURES 1660
abolished Feudal revenue and Knight-service Tenure ; ∴ prepared the way for the *Crown's dependence on Parliament* for Revenue, and for a Standing Army.

TREASON.

The following distinctions are found in its history :—

    High—*Petty* ; **Direct**—*Constructive* ;
    by **Intent**—by *Action* ; **Standing**—*Temporary* ;
    Personal against the King—*Impersonal.*

"**Petty**" treason was the treachery (to a *lord inferior* to the King) of a *wife* **murdering** her Husband, a *servant* his Master, a *priest* his Bishop ; abolished as such 1828.

"**HIGH**" **treason** is a breach of the allegiance owed to the King by a Subject, or by an alien living under his protection.

(i) The *earliest* and *worst* of crimes; beyond mercy, and, when other crimes were compoundable for money, *this* never was.

(ii) The *de facto* King (though a usurper) is the object of it; a *mere de jure* king—*never*.

(iii) The *scope* of it has been defined

    (a) **by Judges** originally, whose servility to covetous Kings led them to pronounce any "*accroachment*" on royal power—" treason "; ∴

    (b) **by Parliament**, esp. by *Statute of Treasons* 1351;

    (c) **by Judges again,** who have widely interpreted that Statute; and, whereas Treason at first was only against the King *personally* (cf. **Strafford's** case 1640), the modern idea is wider.

A. **TREASONS DIRECT**, i.e. by **STATUTE**, plainly interpreted:—

STATUTE OF TREASONS 1351 (25 Edward III) restricted Treason to *seven* forms.

    Treason by *Intent*, i.e.

I. **To compass death** of the **King,** his **wife,** or **eldest son**: the **Intent** is the treason; but an **Overt Act** must also be charged and proved, such as, e.g.,

    (a) *Killing*: ∴ in the **Regicides'** case 1661 the beheading of Charles I proved the " compassing." Or

    (b) *Presence* at a discussion on *How* to Kill: as in case of **Digby** 1606 (Gunpowder Plot). Or

    (c) *Publication* of print or writing: *but*, if only **Unpublished** writing, or **spoken** words?

        Yes, if suggesting a *specific mode* of killing; (and it may, anyway, throw light on *another* overt act);

        else, *not* " overt acts " per se; *yet* court convicted
            Peacham 1615 for an *unpublished* sermon, and
            Sidney 1683, by an *unpublished* essay on the responsibility of Kings, failing a 2nd witness.

[**TREASON ACT** 1817 makes a further Treason by *Intent*—if manifested " by print, writing, or other overt act "—

    viz.: **To compass** even the King's **bodily harm** likely to be fatal, or **wounding,** or **imprisonment**;

    ∴ a **mere conspiracy** to levy war, if *against the King's person*, as above, is now a *statutory* treason *per se*; it *had been* regarded as only

        (i) An *Overt Act* which might prove *Compassing death*;

    or (ii) A "*Constructive*" treason, by Judges.

        Now, if *not* against King's person, it is *treason-felony.*]

Treasons by *Action*, i.e.

II. To violate King's *wife, eldest spinster daughter,* or *eldest son's wife*:

If she consents, she too is traitor; **Anne Boleyn.**
This clause does not cover wives of *junior* princes.

III. To levy war against the King *in his realm*:

directly = *actual rebellion*, or *use of force*, e.g. holding a fort against the King's soldiers;
constructively—has a far wider application, v.i.

N.B. A *mere Conspiracy* (to levy war) *never* constituted *this* treason.

IV. To adhere to the King's enemies, aiding or comforting them, in the realm or *elsewhere*:

"*Enemies*" are *Aliens at War* with us; and this treason is committed **even if** you

(a) give but *trifling* aid, e.g. cook meals for them.

or (b) render aid *outside the realm*; **R. v. Casement** 1916.

or (c) try to get *naturalised* in enemy State; **R. v. Lynch** 1903.

or (d) a resident alien, *join your compatriots*, who "*occupy*" the British district you reside in, e.g. a corner of Natal, as in **De Jager's** case 1903.

But in **R. v. Ahlers** 1915, a German Consul, who helped Germans here to return home and fight, escaped on the plea that he *believed* his *office* justified him.

V. To slay the **Chancellor, Treasurer,** or a **Judge,** during his discharge of his office:

(Now probably would be tried as mere murder.)

But VI. *Forging* the royal *Seals* or *Coinage*:

VII. *Importing* false currency:
have been, since 1861, mere *felonies*.

N.B. Further treasons were created by

1 ANNE :—To maliciously **hinder from the throne** the person next entitled by Act of Settlement.

6 ANNE :—To maliciously **affirm by print or writing**

(1) the *title* of anyone not entitled by Act of Settlement;

or (2) that *Parliament is unable* to fix the succession.

N.B. Temporary Treasons—to meet special situations—were created by Parliament at various times, esp. under the Tudors, e.g. denial of royal supremacy: calling Elizabeth "*usurper*"; and **by 3 Vic.**:—to marry, or effect the marriage of, any child of the Queen under 18, without the proper consents.

B. CONSTRUCTIVE TREASONS :—

The 1351 Statute being **silent** as to a *Conspiracy to levy war*, and **elastic** as to "*War*"—"*against the King*," "*Overt Act*,"

∴ **JUDGES** found openings for wide **extensions,** culminating in those fictions of the 18th century, by which *Treason* appeared *consistent with devotion to the King's person*;

∴ (a) Levying "**War against the King**"

has been held to include the *actual use of Any Force*, e.g. of a mob, or explosives,

if with a **public, universal, national** aim, such as

(i) to subvert the King's Government, or force him to change his counsellors; case of **Essex** 1601;

(ii) to coerce Parliament into legislation; cf. case of **Lord Gordon** 1780;

(iii) to open *all* prisons, expel *all* aliens, or destroy *all* chapels; case of **Damaree and Purchase** 1711.

But if with a merely *private, particular*, or *local* aim, it is only a *Riot*.

(b) "**Compassing death**" **of the King**

was held to be provable by **any Overt Act** (∴ e.g. by the *act* of Conspiring) manifesting an **Intent**

(1) to *Depose* or *Imprison* the King:

or (2) to *Incite* any foreigner to *invade* the realm:

or (3) to *Levy war* for coercing the King, or either House, to adopt new measures.

But Juries, disliking these judicial fictions, were slow to convict; ∴ these (b) 1, 2, 3, "*constructive*," were made **Statutory, treasons** by

the **TREASON ACT** 1795, confirmed **1817.**

But **MODERN LEGISLATION** has tended to **narrow** the scope of Treason; thus

(i) Since the **Riot Act 1715**—a violent political rising, given the statutory conditions, can be prosecuted more conveniently as a *felonious Riot*.

(ii) by **5 Vic.**:—the **Act** of discharging e.g. a gun, or of flinging e.g. a stone, at the Queen, *with intent to injure or alarm her*, is a "high misdemeanour."
This does not exclude a *possible* Treason (**compassing** death or bodily harm) *provable* by such overt act.

(iii) by **Treason-Felony Act 1848**:—the 1817 Act is partially repealed, i.e. the old "*Constructive*" treasons (b) 1, 2, 3, are reduced to *treason-felony* (non-capital), **except** when the "*Intent*" or "*Conspiracy*" is against the **King's person,** as defined in the 1817 Act.

PECULIARITIES in the **TRIAL** of a **Traitor?**
  by Statutes of **1552 : 1695 : 1708.**

As some set-off against the Crown's might and interest arrayed against him—*but* **not if** the charge is a murderous attack on the King's person—

- (a) **2 witnesses** are necessary (1552 : 1695); and, if they testify 2 different overt acts, *both* acts must refer to the *same form of treason.*
- (b) **3 years** is the time-limit for the prosecution of any treason done within the realm. (1695.)
- (c) **10 days before trial,** a copy of the *indictment*, and a list of the *jurors* and *crown witnesses*, must be sent in (1695 : 1708).
- (d) **35** peremptory **challenges** of Jury can be claimed.

PUNISHMENT?

Formerly—*Forfeiture* of all property to the King; and to be *drawn, hanged, disembowelled alive, quartered*; and public *exposure* of remains.
  Last suffered by **Cato St. Conspirators** 1820.

By **Act of 1870** all the above was abolished; death is to be by *hanging*, or, if King signs for it, by the *axe*; but for some treasons the sentence would not be death.

REVOLUTIONS.

In what senses known in English history?
The term has been applied variously to a

A. Non-violent REVERSAL of a NATIONAL TRADITION, e.g. in Economics, Church Status, or Parliamentary Representation, by

  I. A Movement gradual, **undesigned** as a whole,
    see the "*Industrial Revolution*" 1750— ;

or **II. Legislation designed,** and effected *uno ictu,*
    see the "*Reformation*," 1529–1536 : "*Reform Act*" 1832.

B. RE-SETTLEMENT, practically **bloodless,** and directly **designed,**

  Of the **RELATIVE POWERS of the Governing ORGANS ;** without any **structural change ;** but with or without a King's **deposition ;**

  see the *Barons' Oligarchic* schemes, 1258, 1311, 1388; the "*Great Revolution*" 1688.

C. VIOLENT, *substitution* of a new **KING** or **DYNASTY,** without any **structural change ;** but possibly involving some **re-distribution of powers ;**

  see the *Norman Conquest*:
    the *Depositions* of Edward II, Richard II :
    the *White Rose victory*, 1461.

D. VIOLENT CHANGE in the **ORGANIC** structure of the **CONSTITUTION**, which is

    I. **Temporarily Suspended**—without any break in the continuity of private law;
see the "*Civil War*" 1642–1649.

or II. **Permanently Re-cast**—even the private law going into the "melting-pot";
as e.g. *in France* 1789: *Russia* 1918.
England has **never** known **this extreme type**.

    Note :—The "**REVOLUTIONS**" and "**REVOLTS**" of our history were

    (a) in 15*th century*—mainly **DYNASTIC** ;

       (i) The **War of the Roses** was primarily to decide between Yorkist and Lancastrian titles; but, also, in **origin** largely *Social*, ∴ Baronial rivalries;

       in **results** *—*Political*.

       (ii) The abortive **Revolts of Warbeck and Simnel** traded on the Yorkists' hereditary title.

    (b) in 16*th century*—mainly **RELIGIOUS** ;

       (i) The **Reformation,** regarded as a triumph of Lollardism, was *religious*; **but,** as an autocratic coup of Henry VIII, was *political* in motive and in results. And Elizabeth's motives were *more political* than *religious*.

       (ii) **The "Pilgrimage of Grace,"** though inflamed by the fall of the monasteries and of papal supremacy, was founded on *economic* and *political* grievances.

       (iii) The **Puritan movement**—started as a *religious* protest; but soon, by persecution, became *political*.

    (c) in 17*th century*—mainly **POLITICAL** ;

       (i) The **Civil War** was to decide whether *King* or *Parliament* should be supreme;
but, it required religious persecution to kindle it, and became a strife of creeds.

       (ii) The **Great Revolution** was rich in *political results*; but it started in a national *resistance to Popery*.

    (d) in 18*th century*—primarily **ECONOMIC** ;

       i.e. the **Industrial Revolution,** but this had vast *political* and *social* results.*

THE HOUSE OF LORDS.

How was its constitution originally determined?

The Saxon "WITAN" was its forerunner, as being
a **Non-Representative assembly**;
in **Personal** touch with the **King**;
Aristocratic, in sense of **qualified** by *learning, birth, office,* or *tenure,*
to **Advise the King** as to jurisdiction, legislation, etc.

The Norman "MAGNUM CONCILIUM"

was the Witan so *transformed* that its membership,
∴ "*aristocracy,*" depended, at first,
    on **Land-tenure in chief**—as a title *ipso facto*;
but **later** rather on the **King's selection**; for

This "GREAT COUNCIL" CHANGED :—

A. NARROWED gradually, **BY ROYAL SELECTION,** to a **Council of the Great,** i.e. of **BARONS,** the denotation of "**Baron**" passing through these phases :—

  I. Any Tenant-in-Chief, at first;
    but a *distinction* arose *among* tenants-in-chief :—

    (a) "*Barones majores*"—who held a "*baronia*," i.e. over 13 Knights' fees on a single title; dealt with the Exchequer *directly*; and *personally* rendered to the King battle service and advice;
      ∴ were to be summoned each by a *special writ*.

    (b) "*Barones minores*"—who dealt with King and Exchequer only *through the Sheriff*;
      ∴ were summoned only by a *general writ*, sent to Sheriff. These later were *merged with county Knights*, and ceased to be "Barons."

∴ **II.** A *Tenant-in-chief* **who held a baronia,**
    and ∴ could expect a special writ *as a matter of course*.
    But this ceased to be a *matter of course*;

∴ **III.** *Holder of a "baronia,"* **who in fact got a special writ;** whether he *did*—lay in King's discretion.
    Thus **the special writ** became the crucial *test*, and soon an *all-sufficient title*, for "Baronage";

∴ **IV. Receiver of a special writ of summons,** even though he had **no baronia** of land; hence, from 1400 c., the summons ran "*fide et ligeantiâ*," no longer "*fide et homagio*."

  V. *Now* = **Any one entitled** to a **special writ** by office, heredity, or (since 1387) by original patent.

N.B. The term "*Peers*" originated when, in the 14th century, Barons claimed a general right of *trial* by equals (*pares*), but in fact secured this only for their *treason* or *felony*.

N.B. The old principle of *Royal Selection* survives now in the *prerogative* of creating peers, nominating bishops, and trial of a claim to an old peerage.

Also, the King has a *throne*, and *can speak*, in House of Lords, it being **one** of his **advisory Councils.**

B. HEREDITARY CHARACTER attached

never to *Spiritual* peers, i.e. Bishops and Abbots, who, until Tudor times, were a majority of the House;

but to **Temporal** peers, as a result of their old qualification by **tenure**; for as the **tenure** must descend to the "*heir*," so too would the **peerage dignity.**

Yet "**BARONAGE BY TENURE**" was later found to be **inconsistent** with the **hereditary** title to *peerage*; ∴ was declared obsolete in Fitzwalter case 1669: and Berkeley peerage case 1861;

∴ (a) **Land** became **more alienable**;

∴ if peer A sold his *tenure* to X, and X were *thereby* entitled to *peerage*, A's heir would be ousted, and the King's prerogative (to determine peers) invaded.

and (b) a mere **Writ of Summons**, sent to Z by name,

made Z, *though landless*, a **hereditary** peer;
Clifton case 1673;

but only if Z took his **seat**,
Freschville case 1677;

and that in a **full Parliament**,
St. John case 1915.

N.B. The **Hereditary nature** of our temporal Peerage

(i) *Differentiated* House of Lords from Privy Council.

(ii) *Weakened* the real "*aristocracy*" of the House; for the "accident of an accident" need not be "*one of the best.*"

(iii) *Saved us* from a "*caste*" nobility; for only *eldest* sons mature into nobles; our law knows of no nobility "by *blood*," i.e. by *mere* pedigree.

(iv) *Checked* the "*swamping*" of Peers; for a new batch of e.g. *radical* peers might all have *tory* heirs.

(v) Caused the ultimate *rejection of* "Barony by *Tenure.*"

C. DISTINCTION of the "Lords" was MORE MARKED, when

in 13*th century* The **Commonalty** sent **Representatives** to the *One-Chamber* Parliament;

in 14*th century* The Lords became a **Separate Chamber,**

DIFFERING from the House of **Commons**, ∴

I. **Personally** summoned, in their own right, to **Advise**; not *elected*, under a writ to the *Sheriff*, to assent to *taxes.*

II. **Great Landowners** in the main; none in *trade*;

III. **Church Dignitaries** in majority: the rest being **hereditary nobles**;

IV. Exercising the **Jurisdiction** of the King in Parliament;

V. Existing **Continuously**, untouched by a "*Dissolution.*"

D. MEMBERSHIP CHANGED, *after* 1500, by becoming
  (a) more **Lay**—∴ some 36 Abbots ceased to attend, when the monasteries were dissolved.
  (b) more **Royalist**—∴ the Crown ennobled *new men*, the older Baronage having largely disappeared.
  (c) more **Numerous**—temporal peers, about 30 in 1500, were 150 by 1700; 562 by 1820, Pitt having turned them into a *Tory Chamber* by giving peerages to the *wealthy*.
  (d) more **Representative**—of the *public services*; for as the " *Peerage Bill* " 1719 was rejected, and the *prerogative* of creating peers thus *preserved*, a premier can use it to exalt those distinguished in Politics, Law, War, Science, etc., to the position of " *Lords of Parliament*."

N.B. TITLE to a seat in the House of Lords is **NOW** :—
  I. By **Royalty** : ∴ the Sovereign, and royal Princes.
  II. By **Peerage of the United Kingdom** : which rests on
        (i) original *patent* grant, *with* a Writ of *Summons*;
    or (ii) *heirship* either
          (a) to such an original patentee,
        or (b) to some ancestor who once received a bare Writ of Summons, *and* took seat.
  III. By **Election** : as **Representative**
        (a) of the *Scottish peerage*; 16 being elected for each new Parliament since 1707;
        (b) of the *Irish peerage*; 28 sit for life, since 1801.
  IV. By **Office** :
        (i) *Archbishops* 2, *Bishops* 24; but the seat is lost if the see is resigned. No Irish bishops since 1869.
        (ii) The *Lords of Appeal* 6; but these sit as barons for life, even if they resign office.
        (iii) The *Judges*, in theory; but they only attend *by express request*.

THE BARONAGE.

The parts it played until Tudor times ?

A. OPPRESSORS of the people, not *politically*-minded, but each relying on **his own violence,** to defy, in some cases, even the King :
  Such were the **EARLIEST BARONS,** whose ambition provoked
        (a) *anti-baronial policy* of Will: I, Hen: II ;
        (b) rapid advance of *centralised* government.
  But (i) **Chivalry,** a legacy from the Crusades, helped to *humanise* them :
    (ii) **Loss of the French duchies** led to their interests being *focussed on England* :
    (iii) **The Nobility** of high **Officials** infused a new strain, inclining to *law* and *order*, and regardful of *interests wider* than their own ; ∴

B. LEADERS OF CONSTITUTIONAL movements,
in 13th and 14th centuries, for **limiting the Monarchy**:

 I. Conservative at first: see *Magna Carta* 1215; making common cause, with each other, and with the people, against tyranny.

 II. Progressive, in so far as *Montfort* designed a more *representative National* Parliament.

 III. Revolutionary, when prominent Barons, hopeless of *local* independence, tried to snatch the *central* power; and to set up an *Oligarchy*, which would reduce the King to impotence;

  See **Provisions of Oxford 1258.**
   Lords Ordainers 1311.
   Lords Appellant 1388.

In the **Hundred Years' War** the *stay-at-home* Barons, and the Commons, were **harmonious in Parliament,** as a rule. But

 (a) the **warfare** in France—stimulating their plundering instincts:
 (b) their **vast estates**—breeding hot rivalries:
 (c) the **royal connections** of many Barons—

combined to make a large proportion of the Baronage

C. ARROGANT, FACTIOUS, LAWLESS—*in 15th century*:

 I. They **dominated Parliament**—which, until 1437, nominated the **Council,** which ∴ was a Committee of *leading Barons*, too strong for the King.

 II. The **rivalry** of Baronial **factions**

  (a) tended to unsettle the "*personnel*" of House of Lords; ∴ the Commons seemed the more *stable* chamber.

  (b) vented itself in the *dynastic* quarrel, which started the **War of the Roses,** in which many old Baronial families perished;

 III. The remnant—a lawless lot—kept anarchy alive by "**Maintenance**" and "**Livery**":—

  i.e. a Baron's clients could count on his *might*, to "*maintain*" them in any *lawsuit*; ∴ the Courts were terrorised, justice defeated.

   Those who wore his *livery* or *badge* had a special claim to such support, which meant immunity for their iniquities.

  ∴ The "**Statute of Livery and Maintenance**" 1487 created the *Star Chamber*,* to stop this scandal.

D. A RE-CREATED Baronage,
  ∴ **A House of Lords transformed,**
is a conspicuous feature of the Tudor régime;
  (i) **Lay Peers?**—doubled in number by royal creation between 1500 and 1600; ∴ no longer need the Crown fear Baronial opposition.
  (ii) **Spiritual Peers?**—the Crown's right to nominate these was settled at the Reformation.
But, after the awakening of the House of Commons under Elizabeth and James I, we reach the period of **Collisions** between the **two Houses.***

TRIAL BY JURY.

The "**Inquest**"—a **prerogative** of Frankish **Kings,** to call on the local folk to testify, when a *royal* right was in question—
was, as "**RECOGNITION**"—i.e. getting information on oath from *persons conversant* (recognitors)—
  (i) *imported* by William I, who used it for Doomsday survey;
  (ii) *adapted* by Henry II for "finding" facts in Judicial disputes;
  (iii) *developed* in connection with **practices already known** in our law, viz. :—
    (a) *Summons by Sheriff* of County Court.
    (b) *Popular judgments* for doing justice.
    (c) *Presentation* of reputed criminals by Thegns.
    (d) *Representation* of local units, e.g. Hundred, Diocese.
    (e) "*Compurgation*," by which the accused got off, if he got e.g. 12 others to swear to the credibility of his own oath of innocence;
So finally was shaped into a *peculiarly English* **bulwark** of the **Subject's Liberties.** It never so developed in France.

I. CIVIL JURY :—
  (to try whether A *has a right* v. B, e.g. as to Land) dates from Henry II's invention of trial by **ASSISA,** i.e. by men called to sit and "find" upon the
  Issue of Fact apparent in the "*Original Writ*" :—
  (a) if **Writ of Right**—Land-**ownership** being the issue, the parties chose 4 Knights of the district, who chose 12 others; ∴ the 16 sat as "**GRAND ASSIZE.**"
    This was alternative, at B's option, to "*Wager of Battle.*"
  (b) if *a Writ* for testing merely the right of *Possession,* such as "*Novel Disseisin,*" 12 "lawful men" were summoned by Sheriff to sit as "**Petty Assize.**"
  N.B. (i) "*Assisa*" became "**Jurata**" (jury) when sworn to find even on *incidental* issues of fact. Later, Jury was summoned not by virtue of the Original Writ, but by special writ "*Venire facias,*" after pleadings.
    (ii) Juries later were used in **some suits other** than **land**-suits; but **not** for *Debt, Detinue,* nor cases in *Chancery, Admiralty,* or *Star Chamber.*

II. CRIMINAL JURIES :—

(to try whether B is to be punished by the State).

A. JURY OF PRESENTMENT—now our GRAND JURY,

(i) **Anticipated** by Ethelred's law that 12 *sworn thegns* of each Hundred should present suspects.

(ii) **Superseded** "*Compurgation*," after Henry II required Sheriff to summon 12 "lawful men" of each Hundred, to present to a Judge of Assize those locally reputed, or known by them, to be criminals; with a view to *trial by Ordeal*.

(iii) **Popularly elected** at one period, not chosen by Sheriff; e.g. by the "*Iter of* 1194"—by 4 elected Knights choosing 2, who for each Hundred chose 10 Knights.

(iv) **Now** = 16–23 leading men of the County, *summoned* by Sheriff, *charged* by Judge. They *receive indictments*, and decide by majority whether Crown has a prima facie case, to warrant B being placed on trial.

B. PETTY JURY :—a Jury " of Deliverance "—

for *testing* the finding of the *Presenting* Jury; the more needed after the *test by Ordeal* was abolished by Lateran Council 1215.

∴ **12 men of the locality** were summoned by Sheriff;

but (1) B the accused was, in theory, not obliged to *put himself* thus "*on his country*."

∴ (2) if B, objecting, refused to plead, he might until 1772 be persuaded by *Peine forte et dure*, i.e. weights piled on his chest till he agreed; *or died*—thus *escaping* conviction, (and ∴ *forfeiture*) for a felony.

JURY'S FUNCTIONS and QUALIFICATIONS ?

I. Witnesses and **Judges** of *Facts* at first,

relying solely on *their own* knowledge;
∴ had to be *freeholders* of the *Vicinage* (till 1600 c.).

But (a) Consulted later *with others*, out of Court;

(b) "*Afforced*," later, by others better informed;

(c) These *afforcing jurors*, soon after, stood distinct as **Witnesses**;

∴ **Jury** became, about 1450,

II. Judges of *Facts*—on the *evidence of Others*, i.e. of *Witnesses*, taken *in Court*,

and *Unanimity* was required.

∴ No longer selected for their own knowledge 1550 c.
Not to rely on own knowledge without informing the Court 1710 c.

III. **Judges** of **Facts and Law** now :
> they may give a "*General*" Verdict, i.e. on the entire issue ; they are chosen from the *whole county* ; need not be freeholders ; and they are supposed to have *no preconceived ideas* as to the crime charged.

THE JURY'S INDEPENDENCE ?

Formerly obstructed by the risk of

I. **Writ of Attaint :** i.e. Judge could order a re-trial by a *jury* of 24 ; if *their* verdict differed, the first jury suffered arrest, forfeiture and infamy.
> Not abolished until 1825.

II. **Star Chamber,** or King's Bench, **scrutinising** the verdict, especially in *political* cases ; e.g. the jury, which acquitted Throgmorton of treason 1554, were fined and imprisoned.

III. **Coercion** by the **Judge ;** as when he
   - (a) tried to **restrict jury** to the finding of the *facts* ; but Fox's Libel Act 1792 stopped this restriction, *even* in *libel* cases.
   - or (b) **imprisoned jurors** for a verdict against his "*direction*" ; **case of Bushell** 1670 ; one of a jury which acquitted 2 dissenting preachers, "contrary to *direction*" ;
     - ∴ B. was imprisoned. But, on Habeas Corpus writ, was released by Vaughan, C.J. ; for *such* a direction by the judge was improper.

N.B. **Judge** may "**direct**" jury by explaining the relevant law, and weighing the evidence. He may discharge a jury which fails to agree ; and it may be urged, *as a ground of appeal*, that the verdict was "against the weight of the evidence."

POLITICAL interest of the JURY SYSTEM :—

(i) Of the **same parentage** as the *House of Commons*, viz. **Representation** of local communities.

(ii) Illustrates Magna Carta's principle of political justice —the trial "**per judicium parium.**"

(iii) **Security** is provided by it, especially as to *Political* cases,
   - (a) for the **Individual**—against Judges who formerly had an interest in truckling to the Executive ;
   - (b) for the **Government**—against popular odium for a conviction, the conviction being seen to rest on a verdict of "*the country.*"

THE BENCH OF JUDGES.
Their influence on the Constitution?

A. *Mediæval Judges* were
  I. The **King's Agents,** who got to work on the foundations, long before the *Legislature* co-operated;
  ∴ (a) **CENTRALISATION** was advanced by their **circuits,** royal power brought close to the humblest, the barons checked, the Crown fortified.
  (b) **COMMON LAW was nursed** by them, and raised to the prestige of a self-sustained code.
  This helped to *unify* the Nation, to *restrain absolutism*, and was the *foundation* on which the pattern of our later Constitution was to be gradually wrought.
  (c) **CONTINUITY of a "RULE OF LAW"** resulted, unbroken by the fall of a king or a dynasty, generating *respect for precedent*, a *law-abiding* spirit, a sentiment *against revolution*.

  II. **So Dependent on the King** for their office, that often they had to accommodate their rulings to his wishes, e.g. their straining of the law of *Treason* *;
  ∴ Parliament under Edward III checked such subservience; and required an *Oath* from each judge, on appointment, *to heed no royal mandate.*

B. *Tudor Despotism* involved the *degradation* of ordinary *Judges*, ∴ the **Executive** absorbed supreme **Jurisdiction;** the **politician** obscured the *judge.* Hence the *judges* were
  (i) *obsequious*—e.g. legalised Benevolences for Hen: VIII;
  (ii) *unjust*—rarely would a political offender be tried impartially; evidence was twisted to secure a conviction.
  (iii) *undignified*—trials being often wrangles between prisoner, and Judge, who acted as *prosecutor.*

C. *Stuart Judges, of 17th century,*
  could hardly avoid *political partisanship* in the struggle between Parliament and the King, during whose pleasure they held office;
  ∴ I. **Grossly SERVILE, in the main,**
  cowed by the risk of a dismissal like Coke's, they allowed "**Prerogative**" to have a side **superior to all law;** see cases of

Bate 1606	Hampden 1637
Peacham 1616	Jenkes 1676
Darnel 1627	Sidney 1683
Rolle 1629	Godden v. Hales 1686;

  while criticism of the Government was gagged by the Judges, as *Seditious Libel.** But

  II. **SOME Judges,** esp. *Coke,* **vindicated the COMMON LAW;** so the Constitution was upheld in the cases of

Prohibitions * 1608;	*Commendams** 1616;
Proclamations * 1610;	*Seven Bishops** 1687.

D. Since, by *Act of Settlement* 1700,
> they have held **office no longer** "*durante bene placito,*" our **MODERN JUDGES** are more **CONSTITUTIONAL** in their attitude; and, **Because**

>> **I. Not fettered by any written Constitutional Code**—such as *politicians* concoct after a revolution—they have been **FREE TO BUILD UP,** by **Case decisions,** many of our most valued **LIBERTIES,** e.g. of *Public Meeting*; of *Personal Freedom*; Right of *Reputation*; *Freedom of Speech*;
>> thus far our Constitution is a "**part of the Common Law,**" too particularly rooted to be easily uptorn.

>> **II. Independent of the Government** of the day—they have boldly **GUARDED the RIGHTS of the subject, against** action **ultra vires**
>> even of *House of Commons,* see Stockdale v. Hansard;
>> even of a *Minister of State,* see Wilkes v. Wood.

>> **III. Parliament,** being a *Sovereign* body, **can never be said** to legislate **ultra vires,**
>> Judges *here* cannot be asked, as e.g. in U.S.A., whether a Bill would be, if passed, "*Constitutional*";
>> ∴ **our Judges** are peculiarly **DETACHED from POLITICAL bias** and **intrigues;** which helps to explain how

>>> (a) The **justice of British Courts is** conspicuous for its *purity,* so that
>>>> (i) lustre is reflected on the Crown, its fountain;
>>>> (ii) such an example reacts on other official activities;
>>>> (iii) our Colonies have the more readily accepted our empire.

>>> (b) That **spirit of Legalism,** distinctive of our system, makes possible here, as nowhere else, a conflict between
>>>> What the **Judges** declare to be **law**—and
>>>> What the *Government* may tolerate as *expedient*;
>>>> see as to e.g. Martial Law.*

YET our Constitution is NOT WHOLLY Judge-made; it owes much to
> (i) **Conventions,*** developed from political practice;
> (ii) **Statutes,** reflecting the wisdom of philosophers and statesmen, such as

>> *Statute of Tenures:*   *Reform Act:*
>> *Habeas Corpus Acts:*   *Annual Army Act:*
>> *Bill of Rights:*   *Representation of the People*
>> *Act of Settlement:*   *Acts:*
>> *Naturalisation Acts:*   *Parliament Act:*

THE METHODS OF LAW-MAKING.

By what stages has the **House of Commons** secured the **control of Legislation?**

A. *On advice* of the **Magnates,** before the "*Commonalty*" was represented, **THE KING** controlled the *initiation* and *drafting* of

    I. **Constitutions**—to settle points in dispute; e.g. of Clarendon 1164.

    II. **Assizes**—prescribing a form of *procedure*, or some assessment; e.g. of Northampton 1176: of Arms 1181.

    N.B. a **Charter** was a sealed recognition, by the King, of old-established liberties, rarely of new matter; and it might be *initiated* by the Magnates.

B. *With assent* of the **Commons also,** by 1300 c.;

    (i) For *New Taxes*—such assent was to be vital; so said "Confirmatio Cartarum" 1297.

    (ii) In *all measures* of *general interest* the Commons had a right to *concur*; so said Parliament of 1322.

C. *By request* of the **Lords, or** of the **Commons,** when by **PETITION** (1327–1460 c.) either **House** could **initiate** a new measure; but a *Petition* depended on

    (1) the *King assenting*; (2) the *King drafting* as he chose, and *enacting* when he pleased,

a "**Statute**"	or	an "**Ordinance**"
(a) If a matter of *permanent* interest; meant to endure; ∴ more purely Legislative.		(a) If of *temporary* interest, to meet a passing occasion; ∴ rather an Executive act of the Council;
(b) Entered on the *Rolls of Parliament*; repealable only by Parliament.		(b) in form of *Letters Patent* or *Charter*; revocable at King's will.

But   **I.** The need of **concurrence of both** Houses, in the Petitions of *either*, was postponed for a while, esp. as the Lords figured *ambiguously*—as a branch of Parliament, and as the King's Advisers.

    II. The King in Council, *without any Petition*, could **initiate Ordinances,** which, as the Council grew stronger, tended to become *more legislative,* ∵ covering matters proper to Statute-law, or encroaching on the Common Law.

    III. "**Petition**" was **defective** as an overture to legislation, ∵ it might be *shelved*, or the assent *delayed*; or law so *drafted* as to *miss the ratio legis*; or the new law made *subject* to the King's power to "*dispense*" from it, or to *revoke* it; ∴

D. *By authority* of **Parliament** (1460 c.), when a **BILL** was **initiated, drafted** in the form desired, and **passed** by both Houses—**before** reaching **the King,** who at first—could *assent,* or *dissent,* or *mutilate* it; later—must either *assent* or *dissent* in toto; finally—since Anne—must by convention, *assent.*

yet (a) **PARLIAMENT'S AUTHORITY** to legislate was

   (i) **Concurrent** in fact with that of **King in Council,** in 16th and 17th centuries, ∴ often invaded or neutralised by the King's

   Ordinances * :   *Proclamations* * :
   Suspending power * :   *Dispensing power* * :

but (ii) **Exclusive,** after the 1688 Revolution, which stopped such "*Prerogative*" interference, and established the "*Sovereignty of Parliament.*"

and (b) **The PREDOMINANCE of the COMMONS** over the **Lords,** in determining the course of Legislation, was not complete until 1911, though foreshadowed long before :—

∴ (i) **The Commons**

   (a) after the Wars of the Roses *ceased* to look to the *Lords* for *leadership*;

   (b) in the Great Rebellion overbore, and *abolished the Upper House.*

(ii) **The Commons'** Control of **Finance** * involved "*conventions*" which extended that control to measures other than financial; cf. *Tacking.**

(iii) "**Swamping**"—actual or threatened—became a mode of *coercing the Lords* when, with other prerogatives, that of *creating peers* lay virtually in a premier's discretion, e.g. 1711, 1832, 1911.

(iv) **Democracy,** advancing after 1832, involved the

   (a) *reform* and *independence* of the Commons;

   (b) demand for *legislation* in the *interests of* not a privileged class, but *all sections* of the governed—interests more adequately represented in the Commons than in the House of Lords.

   (c) "*Convention*" that the *Lords should yield,* if, on appeal to the country, the Bill they had rejected was popularly approved.

(v) **Parliament Act 1911** * reduced almost to a shadow the Lords' influence on legislation.

THE CROWN'S interference in LEGISLATION

by **prerogative** *real* or *assumed* ?

has taken the form of the "**Executive**"

A. MAKING LAW

I. By "**Constitution**" or "**Assize**" or "**Ordinance**"

  (a) in the *pre-parliamentary* period, when the King in Council was "Executive" and "Legislature" combined;

but (b) when *Parliament* developed as a *separate organ*, it resented the Council's *indefinite* power to **Ordain**, tried to restrict it to occasional executive matters, and claimed to be paramount in law-making—
  a claim not made good until 1688.

II. By "**Proclamations**," which, in the *Star Chamber* * period 1487–1641, tended to *replace* "Ordinances," and exceed their scope, ∴ a mode of legislating on *religion, taxation, trade, press,* and *sumptuary* topics;

  (a) by **Act of Proclamations 1539** a servile Parliament agreed to Proclamations being *as valid as Statutes*, if not prejudicial to subjects' person or property.

  Repealed by 1 *Edward VI*;

  Yet, *legislative* Proclamations were issued by Mary, Elizabeth, and James I, who thus tried to penalise e.g. building near London;

  ∴ "*Creating a new offence*"; hence the

  (b) **Case of Proclamations 1610,**

  in which Coke declared Proclamations to be *unlawful* if *legislative*, lawful only if by way of advertising, or effectuating, existing law.

  Yet Charles I still "*created new offences*" thus; so Coke's ruling was not observed until after the Star Chamber was abolished.

  (c) **Now**—a royal **Proclamation**, or **Order in Council**,

  (i) if *warranted by Statute*,

  may be *legislative*, by delegation from Parliament; such were numerous in the Great War, warranted under **D.O.R.A.**

  (ii) if *not so warranted*,

  it is lawful only if *admonitory* or *administrative*;

  ∴ if it "*created a new offence*," an "**Act of Indemnity**" would be needed, as in 1766, when the Executive by "Proclamation" forbad *export of wheat*.

B. REMITTING the PENALTY, for an **individual** violating Statute, by writ or grant "**non obstante**" that Statute, which *remained law for all others*.

This "DISPENSING POWER" was

I. **Derived** from *Papal usage* 1250 c.; also, when later a *Statute*, made on Petition, was ascribed to the *King's grace*, it would follow that he could *reserve* a power to "*dispense*" from it.

II. **Defensible** on principle inasmuch as
   (a) the King was merely *waiving his own profit*, when the "penalty" was a *fine* or *forfeiture* to the *Crown*;
   (b) the Crown could admittedly *forbear to prosecute* (nolle prosequi), or *pardon*, after conviction, for a *single* offence;
   what was "*Dispensation*" but an "*anticipatory pardon*," covering, however, *repeated* offences?
   (c) the bearing of a new Statute was, then, *not as well foreseen* as now; ∴ a power in the Crown to relieve a case of special hardship was desirable. But

III. **Dangerous** by the **vague extent** of its exercise; common malefactors might thus go unpunished; ∴ attempts *to limit it* were made by *Judges*, who
   (i) **temp. Henry VII**—held that King could dispense *only* as to *mala quia prohibita* (e.g. smuggling), *never* as to *mala in se* (e.g. murder).
   (ii) in **Thomas v. Sorrell 1674**
      T. sued for a penalty ∵ S., of the Vintners Co., sold wine without the licence required by Statute.
      The Vintners Co. had a patent from James I, which *dispensed* it from that Statute;
      held—that a "**Dispensation**" **could cover,**
      (a) if the Statute was for the *Crown's benefit*, even a *continuous* breach of it;
      (b) *otherwise*—only *one* specific breach, and *not that*, if a *subject's rights* are *prejudiced* thereby;
      But it

IV. **Implied a Prerogative** *superior to Law*, as in
   (a) the **Case of "Non Obstante"** (Henry VII):—
      a Statute 1444 had said the King could *not* appoint a Sheriff for *more than* 1 *year*, and *could not dispense* from this;
      yet the Judges held he *could* dispense, because the Statute infringed a *Prerogative*.
   (b) **Godden v. Hales 1686,**
      a collusive suit for a penalty, ∵ H., a *Papist*, held a military *office* in defiance of the *Test Act*. The King had "*dispensed*" him. Servile Judges held the dispensation valid; *but that Act was not for the Crown's benefit.*

The power was freely abused by James II in derogation of the *Test Act*; ∴ was **abolished by the Bill of Rights 1689,**
Except if the Statute in question permits it; and *except* within limits which a general Act *was to* prescribe, but in fact *never did*.

C. **ABROGATING A STATUTE**
so that *for all subjects* it *ceased to be law* :—

This " **SUSPENDING POWER** " was

I. **Assumed**—either from the King's power, when he could legislate by an "*Ordinance,*" to *revoke that* at will ; or from a generalisation of the Dispensing Power.

II. **Unconstitutional**—after Parliament's authority to legislate was established ; for a Society in which *one* organ could enact laws, while *another* could nullify them, would not be "political," ∴ wanting in a "*Sovereign*" proper. Yet

III. **Exercised in fact**

by **Charles II** as to the Navigation Act ; and as to the penal Statutes on religion, which "*Indulgence*" Parliament made him withdraw.

By James II as to the Test Act, and the penal Statutes on religion. But even dissenters saw that the power, if allowed as to *such*, might extend to *any* sort of Statute ;

∴ it was **absolutely** declared **illegal**
(a) by *Judges* in the *Seven Bishops' case* 1687 :
(b) by *Bill of Rights* 1689.

D. **INFLUENCING members** of the Legislature,

with a view to the *passing*, or the *rejection*, of Bills.
George III especially interfered thus :—

(i) with the **Lords**—by personal appeals, and threats of royal displeasure, thus defeating e.g. *Fox's India Bill* ;

(ii) with members of the **Commons**—by manifold bribery, and penalising, with loss of office or pension, those who voted against his policy.

Our modern monarchy is too secluded from active politics for such interference to be possible now.

SUCCESSION TO THE THRONE.

By what principles has it been determined ?

A. **ELECTION**, by the **People** or their **Leaders**, was, at first, the prevailing title to **Kingship, as to an Office,** demanding **personal competence,** more than royal birth ;
∴ e.g. William I was "*elected*" by the Witan :
John's accession was declared to be "*elective.*"

Yet (i) **Blood royal** ever counted for much ; so the *hereditary* principle competed early with the *elective* ; and

(ii) as the **Office** of *ruling* came to be largely **delegated to Ministers,** the old elective principle waned, to re-appear later as the *Parliamentary.* v.i.

B. **HEREDITARY RIGHT** to the Crown
  I. as to a **Family Estate**—developed with the idea of *Proprietary* Kingship, an outcome of feudal *land law*; it governed successions from Henry III to Richard II, and was fully realised under the Tudors.
  II. as to a **Divine Commission**—was dignified later as a *birthright* vested by God in the Stuarts.
  But such a theory was inconsistent with

C. **THE PARLIAMENTARY BASIS** of our modern Monarchy, which is merely **Representative** :—
  anticipated in the old "*Elective*" principle;
  asserted in
  (i) *Depositions* of Edw: II, Ric: II, James II;
  (ii) *Statutes*, often regulating the succession, especially in the Tudor period;
  (iii) *Establishment* of new *dynasties*,
    Lancastrian, Tudor, Stuart, Hanoverian;

  vindicated finally at the *Great Revolution*, and by the *Act of Settlement*, under which,
  I. The **Royalty** of a specified **Family** is seen to depend on Parliament's choice;
  II. The *Title* of the *Individual*, within that family, is determined by the *Common Law* of *heredity*, to operate even as to *females*.

TYPES OF MONARCHY
in English history;
Changes in the conception of the Royal Office?

A. *Norman* :—only a **SUPREMACY** *inter pares*
    over an **inorganic** State;
  The *King*, as one of many companion warriors, was Commander, Landlord, Judge *in chief*;
  but his absolutism, stark and personal, rested rather on **Might** than on *Law*.

B. *Plantagenet* and *Lancastrian*
  Kingship was a **Supreme OFFICE**
    (i) related *legally* to other *organs* of a *body-politic*:
    (ii) exalted by *Prerogatives*, formulated by *lawyers*:
    (iii) subject to some *limits*, imposed by *Parliament*.
  Thus our King was becoming a "*Rex Politicus*."
  But a reaction against this tendency started 1461; ∴

C. *Tudor* **Kingship** was **PROPRIETARY** and **PATERNAL** :
  England was a pawn he could stake in war:
  The *Crown* a possession he could devise by will:
  Treaties were his personal affairs, lapsing at his death.
  Despotism was no longer *checked*, but **veiled, by Law.**

D. *Stuart* **Kings** pretended a **DIVINE COMMISSION**;
∴ a power *above* and *outside* the body-politic;
∴ Prerogative irresponsible, not limitable by Law.
Such a King was the *reverse* of a "*Rex Politicus.*"
But, as a result of the Great Revolution,*

E. *Hanoverian* **King** was to revive the "**Rex Politicus**"; **PARLIAMENTARY** in title, **CONSTITUTIONAL** in activities; *prerogatives* were still, mainly, for his *personal* exercise, though *some* were beginning to be handled by *Ministers*.

F. *Modern Monarchy* is **REPRESENTATIVE** :—
The Crown is a symbol of imperial unity; and
The King, being an **agent**, has no official will but that of his **principal**, i.e. of the Nation's Ministers and Parliament.
And the **Crown's "demise,"** involving only a change of Agent, has no longer any effect on *Treaties*, on *Parliament's* existence, or on *Judges'* Commissions.

IMPEACHMENT.

A procedure, involving a **trial**, in which the

ACCUSED X may be a **peer**, whatever the offence;
or a **commoner**, if the offence is of State importance;

ACCUSERS are the COMMONS;
a motion by some **M.P.** being first carried, he notifies this to the House of Lords; the Commons, in committee, formulates "*Articles*," and appoints "*Managers*" to conduct the case, if it comes to trial.

JUDGES of law and fact are the **PEERS**,
Lord High Steward presiding if X is a peer:
Lord Chancellor presiding if X is a commoner.

N.B.
(a) **If X is a commoner,** it is not a "trial by his *equals.*"
(b) The question of **guilt** is put to each peer in turn, who stands, uncovers, and with left hand on heart answers "guilty" (or "not guilty") "*on my honour.*"
(c) If the **trial** is so **prolonged** that the peers attending have fluctuated greatly, the House of Lords will decide who are entitled to vote.
(d) **Verdict** of the **majority** is taken; but no *sentence* follows unless requested by the *Commons*, who ∴, by not requesting it, *can virtually pardon* X.

A. TO ENABLE PARLIAMENT, at first, to **FORCE the KING** to **part with a bad Minister,** in the days when
  (i) the King *chose and retained Ministers* at his will;
  (ii) the *Criminal Law* might *not* cover the misconduct;
  (iii) ordinary *Judges* were *too royalist* in sympathy to be relied on in such a case.

I. **Invented 1376** by the "Good" Parliament, against Lord **Latimer, Neville** and **Lyons,** for financial trickery; soon, used freely against e.g. in 1386 **Earl of Suffolk**: 1388 the **Judges** who supported Ric: II: 1450 **Duke of Suffolk** for treachery in France.

II. **Discontinued** from **1450 to 1621,**
∵ Tudor Parliaments were too servile to dare it; and a "*Bill of Attainder*" was a swifter means of removing a Minister, of whom King and People were tired.

III. **Revived 1621,** with *Parliament's* resumption of *independence*, it proved a mighty weapon in the fight against autocracy; (Charles himself tried to turn it against Pym; but, *King* cannot *impeach*.)
∴ **17th century** saw about **40 impeachments,** against Crown **Ministers;** and some **others** (e.g. *Mompesson, Fitzharris, Blair*; and later, *Sacheverell, Hastings*),

notably those of:—

Sir G. Mompesson 1621—for *frauds* as a trade *monopolist*, i.e. a Crown grantee. He was convicted.

Lord Chr. Bacon 1621—for taking *bribes*; convicted and fined; later pardoned by King James.

Lord Middlesex, Treasurer, 1623—for *corruption* over the wine duty; convicted; and the peers resolved that in such misdemeanours X may have *Counsel* to defend him.

Duke of Buckingham 1626—for *bad advice*, and *incompetence*, e.g. in the assault on Cadiz; defeated by "*Dissolution.*"

Lord Strafford 1640—for alleged "*cumulative Treason*," esp. conduct in Ireland, and a speech in Council; but it was dropped, in favour of a "Bill of Attainder."

Abp. Laud 1640—for the "*treason*" of *subverting* the laws, esp. *Protestantism*. But the Judges advised the peers this was not "treason";
∴ a "*Bill of Attainder*" was passed instead.

Lord Clarendon 1667—on a general charge of "*treason*," which was held to be *too vague*; ∴ more precisely charged with e.g. helping Charles to ignore Parliament, and sell himself to Louis. He was exiled.

Lord DANBY 1679—for a *letter* he wrote, by the King's order, proposing that *Louis should buy our neutrality* in a war by France on Holland.
He was in prison nearly 5 years; then the case lapsed by a "*Dissolution.*"

Constitutional points raised in this case?
(i) The *charges* must be *specific*, not vague, as e.g. that he "betrayed the honour" of England.
(ii) *Royal orders* are *no plea* for a Minister impeached.
(iii) *Royal Pardon* is *no bar* to an impeachment.
(iv) *Bishops*, in a *capital* case, may sit and vote in the preliminary stages, but *retire before verdict*.

(v) *Dissolution* ?? Will this defeat a pending impeachment? The peers gave conflicting decisions. See later cases of Hastings and Melville, which decided *it will not.*

Mr. Fitzharris 1681—for *treasonable libel*, the Commons wished to impeach; but he being a *commoner* and the offence *capital*, the Peers refused to violate Magna Carta by such a trial.

The Commons held their refusal a " *breach of Privilege.*"

Sir Adam Blair 1689—for the *treason* of publishing a proclamation of James II, who was dethroned: though he was a *commoner*, and the crime *capital*, yet the Peers heard the case, later opinions discredit this precedent.

B. **As a WEAPON OF PARTY WARFARE—after 1690**, when *royal autocracy* was *no longer to be feared*, it was used, to **punish** or **discredit political opponents**,

by *Tories*—against the Whig lords **Portland, Somers, Orford,** and **Halifax** 1701 for their policy as to the Partition Treaties;

but the Commons failed to proceed with it.

by *Whigs*—in the cases of

(1) **Dr. Sacheverell** 1710—for his *sermons* against Whiggery; he was convicted; but the Whig Ministry of Sunderland fell as the result.

(2) **Lord Oxford** 1715—for *Jacobite intrigue*; but the proceedings were abortive.

(3) **Lord Bolingbroke** 1715—for *similar intrigues*; he was struck off the peerage roll, and banished.

(4) **Warren Hastings** 1788–95—for *extortions*, etc., in India: an indirect attack on Pitt, his patron.

He was acquitted, but ruined in purse by the prolonged trial.

(5) **Lord Melville** 1804—for *peculation* at the Navy Treasury. He was censured, but this was reversed 1807.

In (4) and (5) *Statutes* were passed, to declare that a " *Dissolution* " was *not* to defeat the procedure.

C. **DORMANT** now since 1804, **being SUPERFLUOUS,**

∴ I. for **Criminality,** e.g. corruption by a high official, our ordinary *Criminal Law* is *adequate*; and *Judges* can be *relied on* to be unbiassed.

II. for **Bad Policy**—the Commons can more simply displace a Minister, by vote of censure;

∴ there is no chance of the King retaining a minister the nation has ceased to trust.

It might be revived against some high official, not directly responsible to the Commons. The U.S.A. constitution still retains it.

" BILL OF ATTAINDER ? "

A legislative act : *hardly* a form of *Trial*; for *evidence* was, in some cases, *not heard*; but—that X was guilty, should suffer death, and leave no lawful heirs—was *voted* by both Houses, and confirmed by the Crown ; ∴ became an **" Act."**

It was used for removing

The **Despensers** 1321: Thomas **Cromwell** 1540: **Strafford** and **Laud** 1641: lastly, Sir J. **Fenwick** 1696.

" Bill of Pains and Penalties " was similar ;

but the penalty was *not death*, and the *heirs* were *not disinherited*.

PERSONAL FREEDOM.

How has " Liberty of the Subject " been secured ?

Not positively declared by Statute as a **substantive** right; though Magna Carta required a *tyrannical King* to respect it; but it is secured by **Procedure**

available at *Common Law*,
reinforced by *Statutes* :—

I. *By Common Law*—

by various proceedings, X, the imprisoned, could

(a) get a **Provisional release**—by a **Writ to Sheriff**—
e.g. *Writ de odio et atiâ* = that, if X were detained on a *murder charge*, and Sheriff found charge malicious, X was to be released on bail.

or e.g. *Writ of Mainprize* = to release X, subject to sureties for his appearance on a given date.

(b) have **Legality** of his detention **tested,** even if an alien, with the **chance** of a final **discharge ;**

This by a **" HABEAS CORPUS " WRIT,**

a **" prerogative "** Writ, from King's Bench, addressed **to the Gaoler,** that he *bring up X personally* before the Court, and make a *" return,"* i.e. state the ground of X's detention.

But this Writ might **often** prove **ineffective,**

∴ (i) Gaoler could wait for a *repeated* service ;

or (ii) X's *prison* might be *changed* ;

or (iii) *Not* issuable in Law *vacation* ;

or (iv) Could not operate if X were imprisoned " *beyond the seas* " ;

or (v) Stuart Judges were satisfied with the " return "—
" *by the King's special command* "; as in **Darnel's** case 1627; and inclined to refuse the writ, if X was imprisoned by order of the *Council*, cf. **Jenkes'** case 1676.

∴ Statutes corrected such defects v.i.

(c) **If illegal**—then, for "**False Imprisonment,**" X can

(1) **Prosecute** for this crime;

or (2) **Sue** civilly
to get *damages* for the tort,
which may be "*exemplary*,"
Leach v. Money;
or to get his *freedom declared*, if he were a reputed slave.

II. *By Statutes*
supplementary safeguards have been added;

by **A. PETITION OF RIGHT, 1628 :—**
The **King** is to abandon imprisoning for no offence.

B. ACT of LONG PARLIAMENT 1641 :—

(i) **Even if** X is detained by order of **the Council,** the gaoler's "**return**" must state a **legal** ground.

(ii) **Impressment** for military service was declared **illegal,** *unless* enemies *invade* the realm.

C. HABEAS CORPUS ACT 1679 :—

When X is imprisoned, *not* as a *convict*, but to await his trial on a **criminal charge**

I. of **Treason** or **Felony**—*no writ* avails him *under this Act*, but he must be **tried** at the **Next Assizes.**

II. of **Misdemeanour**—

(a) The **Writ shall issue,** even in vacation, even to run in the Channel Isles, on a written complaint, and view of a copy of the committal warrant.
Judge, refusing it, to forfeit £500 to X.

(b) **Return** to be made by gaoler within 20 days; else, he forfeits to X £100, and loses office; so, too, if he changes X's prison.

(c) **The Court** shall remand, release, or admit X to bail.

(d) Imprisonment of X "**beyond the seas**"? Anyone privy to this shall forfeit £500 to X, be guilty of "*præmunire*," and beyond royal pardon.

This Act was **defective** ∴

(i) *No limit* was set to *Bail*.
∴ Bill of Rights 1689 said "*not to be excessive.*"

(ii) The "return" if good in *law*, though false in *facts*, could not be scrutinised.

(iii) Imprisonments *apart* from any *Criminal charge* were not within its scope.
∴ (ii) and (iii) were corrected by

D. HABEAS CORPUS ACT 1816 :—

If, by *anyone*, X is detained, on **no criminal charge,** but e.g. in a nunnery, asylum, school, ship, or if the true "*guardian*" of X claims custody of X—

(a) The **Writ may issue,** on affidavit showing reason to suspect illegality ;
(b) **Appeal,** if writ is refused, lies to Court of Appeal ;
(c) **Truth of facts** stated in the return *may be scrutinised* by the Court ;
(d) It is "**Contempt of Court**" if gaoler ignores writ.

(So now also as to the 1679 Act.)

CONSTITUTIONAL INTEREST of these Habeas Corpus Acts?

I. **They secure,** as to the imprisonment of anyone (even an alien), unless a *convict*, or charged with *treason* or *felony*, a **scrutiny by K.B.D.** of its legality.

II. **A "Suspension" of the Acts,** by Parliament, is possible, as in e.g. 1780, 1797, 1817, so that the *Executive* is *more free* in coping with a riot or rebellion ; **then,** *only* the benefits *of the Acts* are in abeyance, ∴ *esp.,* prisoner rebels would have *no* right to a "*trial at the next Assizes.*"

III. This **Habeas Corpus Writ** is **typical** of those quickly available **Remedies,** which, as Dicey says, reflect the influence of *Lawyers*, and are a surer *guarantee of the reality* of our *rights* than a mere declaration of "*droits guarantis*" in a paper code ; and

IV. The **supremacy of our Judges** over the *Executive* is conspicuously illustrated by proceedings on the Writ ; e.g. a *Secretary of State* may have ordered the detention of X : the **Court** may order his release.

REVENUE—TAXATION.

I. Originally **ALL REVENUE was ROYAL,**
and the **King** was **no trustee,** but spent, as he chose,

A. ORDINARY Crown Revenue, *Permanent, Hereditary,*
from (i) *Feudal* dues :
(ii) Royal **demesnes** * :
(iii) **Jurisdiction,** i.e. fees and fines ; but, for these, Sheriff might pay Crown a fixed composition—"*ferm of the shire.*"
(iv) **Customs**—i.e., by "prerogative," tolls on merchants' exports and imports ; but *usage* tended to settle the *amount.*
(v) **Sundry** other **prerogatives,** e.g. *escheats.*

But such income proved inadequate, i.e. the King could not "*live of his own*" ; hence the need for

B. **EXTRAORDINARY** Revenue—*Occasional*—**raised by TAXATION.**

I. **Without Consent,** at first; often **at King's will**;

Indirect taxes (esp. Customs) rested on "*prerogative.*" *Direct* taxes were *not so* warranted, but were

(a) on **Land** :—
  (i) "*Danegeld*"—"*hidage*," later "*carucage*," which Witan had legalised; ceased 1250 c.;
  (ii) "*Scutage*," a composition for war service;
  (iii) "*Talliage*"—a poll-tax on tenants in royal demesnes; purely arbitrary, and most resented. Abolished 1340.

(b) on **Personalty ?**—**none,** until "*Saladin tithe*" 1188, i.e. 10 %, by consent of the Great Council; thenceforth, a greater insistence on

II. **Consent,** as essential to warrant **Direct** taxes; e.g. for any *extra* "aid or scutage," by Magna Carta; and the several groups, Barons, Clergy, Knights, Burgesses, voted *severally* the sums they *chose to* contribute; and

II. **REPRESENTATIVES of the COMMONALTY,** in 13th century, being called to **PARLIAMENT,** esp. **to assent to taxes,** a **CONFLICT** begins, which lasts till the 17th century, between

(a) Taxation by **Parliamentary grant;**
(b) Taxation by **Prerogative;**

reflected in e.g. *Confirmatio Cartarum* 1297.

A. **DIRECT** taxes—*a charge, inevitable, on the payer*—were **granted** by Parliament, **Occasionally** :—

(i) *One-fifteenth* on personalty—until 1600 c.

or (ii) "*Subsidy*"—from 1350 c. to 1665 c.

i.e. 4/- in the £ on *land*, 2/8 on *personalty*; later fixed at £70,000; two or more might be voted. Abandoned in favour of *indirect* taxes.

B. **INDIRECT** taxes—*can be "passed on" to consumers, or avoided by forgoing the benefit they purchase* :—

Parliament strove to **withdraw these** from the sphere of "**Prerogative,**" and to "grant" such to the King for a *term*, or for his *life*, or as *hereditary*;

(1) **CUSTOMS** :—i.e. on *exports* and *imports*; formerly

(a) **Antiqua,** magna, **Custuma**—on the *staple* exports, esp. wool: fixed by Parliament in 1275;

(b) **Prisage**—i.e. 10 % of wine imported; later merged in (a);

(c) **Nova,** parva, **Custuma**—specially negotiated by the King with foreign merchants, as by *Carta Mercatoria* 1302,

 to leave no excuse for which,

(d) **Tunnage** and **Poundage**—i.e. *extra* duties on imports and *non-staple* exports—were *granted by Parliament*, from 1373, as a subsidy to each king, *usually* for his *life*; until Anne's reign.

After 1815 Customs were vastly increased, and were paid on some 1200 articles;

"**Free Trade**" involved the abolition of all, except on a few imports.

N.B. As to **collection** of Customs—anciently it was "*farmed out*" e.g. to Italian bankers; but since 1690 c. has been controlled by *Commissioners*. As to **assessment**—once on the *merchants' own valuation*; but, under Mary, Elizabeth and the Stuarts, by "*Books of Rates.*"

(2) **EXCISE :**—paid by **manufacturers** and **retailers** of esp. *beer, cider, wine, whisky*;

(a) started by the Long Parliament 1643:

(b) granted as "*hereditary*" to the Crown 1661, but this is now *surrendered* by each king:

(c) preferred to Customs by Walpole and Pitt, that *smuggling* might be *discouraged*.

Now enlarged, to include even all **Licences.**

III. MODERN REVENUE system dates from 1660–1700, when **Parliament** took full control, and "**Royal**" and "**National**" revenues were distinguished.

It **DIFFERS** from **the ancient,** in respect of its

A. Purposes :—no longer merely to fill a King's purse, or to protect our trade; but to pay for

(i) interest on the *National Debt* * :

(ii) cost of *Government* :

(iii) cost of the *Royal Establishment*.

B. Sources :—

Some old sources being now *extinct*, viz. :—

 Feudal dues—since 1661 :

 Subsidies—since 1665 :

 Customs—mostly cancelled by Free Trade :

 Hereditary Excise—waived, as such, by Crown :

∴ **Now relied on** chiefly are

I. *Taxes* :—*direct*, on Income : on Land : House duty : Death duties ;

 indirect, i.e. Excise, and some Import Customs.

II. *State Monopolies* :—esp. Postal, and Stamps.

III. *Crown's old hereditary*, esp. Royal Demesnes.*

C. **The Consolidated Fund,*** since 1787, i.e. the *reservoir* of revenue, fed by B I, II, III, and standing to the Exchequer's credit at Bank of England ;

Payments IN—are mainly under *standing* Acts ; but Income Tax and Import duties are legalised by *annual* "Appropriation Act" ;

Payments OUT are either

(i) "*Consolidated Fund services,*" by standing Acts, i.e. for National Debt interest, Civil List, and Judges' salaries ;

or (ii) "*Supply services*"—i.e. for naval, military, and executive civil payments—under *C.F. Acts* and the *annual Act*, which place limited sums at the disposal of Ministers ; then the King, by sign manual, authorises Treasury to issue credits.

D. **Permanence** of Taxation :—now necessitated by our National Debt ;* *no longer* would a subsidy "*now and then*" meet our liabilities.

E. **ALL REVENUE** now being primarily **NATIONAL : House of Commons** controls its collection, appropriation, and auditing ; and

The King is

(i) Salaried by a "**Civil List**" * ;

(ii) **Trustee,** for the nation, of the old *hereditary Crown revenue*, with trifling exceptions :

yet (iii) **Capable**—since 1800—of **owning** and **willing** any property, like a private person.

The ROYAL DEMESNES ("*Terra Regis*").

I. **Derived** from "*folcland*" **appropriated** by **William I** as hereditary Crown land ; increased later, e.g. by forfeitures, and at one time nearly one-fifth of England.

No King could *will away* such ; but,

II. **Aliened** often, *inter vivos*, to favourites by wasteful Kings, who, thus impoverished, had ∴ to beg for taxes ;

∴ **Resumed** often by Parliament, e.g. 1450, 1700 ; and by 1 Anne no more title than a 31 *year lease* was to be granted of such lands.

III. **Earmarked by Parliament** 1689 as one of the sources for feeding the "*Civil List.*"

IV. **Surrendered** to the nation, since 1760, by each King *for his reign,* as part consideration for the *Civil List*;

∴ **Administered** now under the Board of Agriculture, they yield about £500,000 a year to the *Consolidated Fund.*

CONTROL OF FINANCE.

By what stages has the House of Commons secured it?

A. PARLIAMENT gradually **WITHDREW FROM** the **KING** the *raising* and *spending* of **Revenue** *at will*:—

by (1) **Declaring against Arbitrary Taxation;**

see (i) *Magna Carta*, as to the Barons' assent;
  (ii) *Confirmatio Cartarum*, as to the Nation's assent; and "*De Tallagio non concedendo*" 1297;
  (iii) *Petition of Right* 1628—the King was to abandon at least *direct* arbitrary levies;
  (iv) *Long Parliament* 1641, as to e.g. Ship-money;
  (v) *Bill of Rights* 1689.

(2) **Substituting Parliamentary grants** for levies by "*Prerogative*," or making the **grant conditional** upon the abolition of e.g. Talliages 1340.

(3) **Resuming royal demesnes** which the King had wastefully given away.

(4) **Appointing Treasurers** to take charge of, and **Auditors** to account for, monies *voted*.

(5) **Inventing new sources**, e.g. *Excise*, and revising these —and the *Customs*—from time to time.

(6) **Abolishing feudal dues** 1660—so making the King dependent on a Parliamentary allowance.

(7) **Appropriating Supplies,** e.g. in 1689; now annually;
∴ the King's Ministers can no longer spend as much as they like, on whatever they choose.

B. THE COMMONS gradually **EXCLUDED THE LORDS** from *initiative, control, interference*, in **finance** :—

I. by **Conventions,** fortified by "**Resolutions,**" and generating a so-called "**Privilege,**" so that

(a) *Money-Bills* could be *initiated* only in the Commons;
(b) "*Money-Bill*" was given the *widest interpretation*;
(c) *No amending*, of such a Bill, by the Peers, was to be tolerated 1671;
(d) *No rejection*, of such a Bill, by the Peers, was to be tolerated 1860.

II. by **Statute 1911 "Parliament Act"** :—

Any *Finance* Bill, *certified* to be such by the *Speaker*, and sent up to the Lords, shall, if the Lords do not assent within *one month*, become Law by the Royal Assent.

END OF VOL. I.

INDEX OF CONTENTS

PERIOD I

(1066—1272)

	PAGE
William I's policy	11
Henry II's reforms	19
Magna Carta	27
Henry III: Montfort's movement	31
Administrative System, Norman and Angevin	35
Church and State in 11th, 12th, 13th centuries	37
Political Influences of 13th century	39

PERIOD II

(1272—1461)

Edward I	45
Parliament—Origin of House of Commons	51
The Three Estates	55
Mediæval Parliament, contrast with Modern	57
Edward III	61
Hundred Years' War—Its effects	65
Church in 14th century	69
Fourteenth Century summarised	71
Henry IV	73
Wars of the Roses—results	75
Royal Council—early history	77
Fifteenth Century—constitutional interest	81

PERIOD III

(1461—1603)

Tudor Monarchy—its strength	85
Henry VII	89
Henry VIII's foreign policy: the Reformation	93
Elizabeth—objects of her policy, etc.	101
Tudor Rule—its advantages	113
Tudor Policy—bearing on next century	115
Star Chamber	117
Court of High Commission	119

PERIOD IV

(1603—1688)

	PAGE
Stuart Despotism—contrasted with Tudor	125
James I's Despotism	127
James I's Reign—its constitutional interest	131
Charles I	133
Long Parliament's work	139
Great Rebellion—Causes—Effects	141
The Privy Council 1461—1641	147
The Commonwealth	149
Why did Cromwell fail?	151
Charles II—motives of his policy	153
The Constitution at the Restoration	155
Foreign Relations under Charles II	157
James II—events leading to the Revolution	161
Revolution of 1688—its importance	171

Puritanism as a force in Politics	175
Feudal Land Law	177
Treason	179
Revolutions as known in England	187
House of Lords—early history of	191
The Baronage—until the Tudor period	195
Jury System	199
Judges—influence on the Constitution	205
Methods of Law-making	209
Crown's interference with Law-making	213
Succession to the Throne	217
Types of Monarchy	219
Impeachment	221
Personal Freedom	227
Revenue and Taxation	231
Control of Finance by House of Commons	239

For Product Safety Concerns and Information please contact our EU representative GPSR@taylorandfrancis.com
Taylor & Francis Verlag GmbH, Kaufingerstraße 24, 80331 München, Germany

www.ingramcontent.com/pod-product-compliance
Lightning Source LLC
Chambersburg PA
CBHW062143300426
44115CB00012BA/2025